THE DOCTOR'S BEST LOVE STORY

By

Walter Lewis Wilson, M. D.

Author of "The Romance of a Doctor's Visits," "Miracles in a Doctor's Life," etc.

"The Doctor's Best Love Story" by Walter Lewis Wilson, M. D.
Copyright 2024 by The Old Paths Publications

Originally Published 1936 by
The Bible Institute Colportage Association of Chicago
843-845 North Wells Street, Chicago

Republished 2024 by
The Old Paths Publications, Inc
www.theoldpathspublications.com
TOP@theoldpathspublications.com

ISBN 979-8-9912642-6-6

Revised Cover by The Old Paths Publications, Inc.

Printed in the United States
2024

Publisher's Comment

Dr. Wilson (1881-1969) was a colleague of mine who destroys the "easy believism" popular during my lifetime. Yet, he presents the fact that to be saved is NOT difficult but is absolutely dependent upon a personal faith in the Lord Jesus Christ, Who loves you with an eternal love. Reading this book will fill your heart with great joy.

Please forgive any formatting errors that occurred during scanning. Thank you.

Dr. Walter Lewis Wilson (1881-1969)

INTRODUCTION

THE whole world knows this love story, at least wherever the Scriptures have gone, and minions have believed it unto salvation. The writer trusts that he is not presuming upon the intelligence of any reader when he offers a series of messages on this precious and wonderful portion of God's Word. True, many sermons have been preached concerning it, and probably no other verse in all the Scriptures has been so often repeated, nor so widely believed.

It is not claimed that all the outlines and suggestions given herein are original. The thoughts expressed have been obtained in part from various sources and, were it possible, credit would be given to each one who has helped in the formation of these messages. The writer is grateful to each contributor and any blessing received by the readers will be manifested at the judgment seat of Christ, so that everyone shall be rewarded according to his own work.

May the gracious Holy Spirit cause this beautiful story of God's love, as revealed in JOHN THREE SIXTEEN, to give forth fresh milk for thirsty, hungry hearts through these pages.

Walter Lewis Wilson
Kansas City, Missouri.

TABLE OF CONTENTS

FOREWORD

This verse, **John 3:16** *"For God so loved the world, that he gave his only begotten Son, that whosoever believeth in him should not perish, but have everlasting life"* has been called "THE GOLDEN TEXT of THE BIBLE." It is indeed golden because of its purity, its heavenly character, and its universal value to man. It has also been called "THE GOSPEL IN A NUTSHELL." Well it may be thus termed, for the great doctrines of the Word are incorporated in the narrow compass of these twenty-five words.

Others have applied to this verse the title "A MINIATURE BIBLE." it is not thus miscalled, for in this passage you find the opening up of God's heart and the revelation of man's need, together with the sufficient remedy. This is the outline of the entire Bible.

This verse may be described as "GOD'S TREASURE CHEST." In these few words there is presented the sweetest treasure of all, for the greatest need of all, and this treasure is sufficient for all.

Since we are told to *"desire the sincere milk of the word,"* in this short passage we may find an everlasting supply of milk, and cream, too. Each time it is approached, a new and fresh portion may be received for the heart.

The drill may bore deep herein for the wonderful supply of oil, and every believer may enjoy a fresh anointing. The sage may ponder over the depths of its meanings, and the child may rejoice in its simple message.

A Message to the Preacher

It is to be observed that John 3:16 was not given to a drunkard, nor to a bandit, nor to any other criminal, but rather was given to Nicodemus, a great teacher of Jerusalem, a central figure in the religious life of the Jews.

Therefore, this is Christ's charge to the public servant. This is Christ's counsel and advice to those who would stand between God and men. This is Christ's reproof to one who is busily engaged in leading the religious thought of his day, but is neglecting to feed God's people with the milk and honey of the Word.

Nicodemus was instructing the people in laws and ordinances, in tithes and regulations, but was not giving the people that which would transform their lives, nor empower them to be what they should be. He was teaching the letter of the law and instructing them in the Mosaic economy, but he was leaving them dead in their sins.

It is as though Jesus said, "Nicodemus, you are telling the people about sacrifices, but they need to know the Saviour. I know you love the people and are giving them the best you have, but when God loved the people, He gave them Christ. You do likewise!"

God grant that every preacher, teacher, and religious leader may be an imitator of God and give Christ Jesus to the people, as he ministers in the Word.

CHAPTER I

FIVE GREAT MIRACLES IN JOHN 3:16

THE Bible is a book of miracles. Both the Old and New Testaments are filled with strange and unusual revelations of God's power in nature and in His dealings with men. One might hardly expect to find any miracles in such a verse as John 3 : 16, but even there miracles are revealed, as they are in many other portions of God's Word. May these unusual revelations of God's greatness stir your heart to love Him deeply and to trust Him more fully.

The Miracle of a Universal Love

No one in all the world could possibly love everyone in the world. Most folk find it quite difficult to love all of their relatives. Perhaps the most bitter of all hatreds is that which exists in families among those who should love each other the most. But God has found it possible, with His great heart of love, to love every individual in the entire world, in spite of his faults. How supreme must be His love which enables Him to overlook all those things which we magnify in human lives, and love faulty people! We find a sort of satisfaction in having likes and dislikes, in nursing loves and hatreds. There are those who all their lives cherish ill will towards someone who in their judgment has injured them.

Here is the great miracle of the universal love of our loving God. He does not love as we love, but He does love those whom we love. He does not love for a little while and then become an enemy; He loves with an eternal love. He does not love because He sees something in us that He can love. He only loves because we need His love and He would have us enjoy the benefits of it. He does not love because He expects to receive something in return. We love in that manner. We love those who love us. We love those who will give us that which our hearts crave and desire. God loves those who are quite unable to return anything to Him, except perhaps the love of their hearts and the praise of their lips. We cannot give Him gold, for He made it; we can only return it to Him when He lends it to us. We cannot enrich Him with a life of service, for the strength to do it and the knowledge and wisdom necessary are gifts from Him. We can only return them to Him because they are His. How matchless is His wonderful and marvelous love which knows no national limits, no racial boundaries, and no social distinctions! He loves You. He loves you just because He loves You. What a miracle is this!-

The Miracle of a Universal Gift

It is indeed a miracle that God should find one gift for every kind of person. Our gifts must be varied and suitable in each individual case. We do not give to the aged grandfather that which we give to the little baby. The gift to the wife is different in character from the gift to a casual friend. But God has found a gift which pleases and satisfies and supplies the need of every living person between the cradle and the grave. God gives to the Eskimo the same gift that He gives to the railroad president. He has the same gift for the children that He has for their parents. The same gift is suitable for the heathen in the darkness of Central Africa and for the banker in the heart of North America Other gifts fade and fail with the passing of time, but this gift grows brighter and more beautiful as the years go by. Other gifts adorn only the outward appearance of the recipient, but this gift fills the life with sweetest graces, as well as adorning the body with calm and composure.

Other gifts change in their value with the customs of the day. They get out of date and out of fashion. But He adorns and satisfies the heart in the twentieth century the same as He has in all other centuries. Sometimes gifts are given which do not please the one to whom they are given. The color is not satisfactory, or the quality is not what it should be, or it does not fit. But no one who has once received Him, has ever found fault with Christ. The miracle of this gift is that He always satisfies and rejoices every heart who receives Him.

The Gift of a Universal Faith

There is only one thing in all the world that every human being can do and that is to believe. God found one thing which could be done by every human being from infancy to maturity. The rich can believe and so can the poor. The sick and weak can trust, and so can the strong and well. The blind can receive and so can those who see. The uneducated can believe and the educated can do no more. God asks for faith. a true faith, a living faith, a faith that believes His Word. He does not ask for money, for many have none. He does not ask for service for salvation, because the sick, the weak, and the aged cannot serve. He does not ask merit for salvation, for no one has sufficient merit to be entitled to such a large payment as the Gift of heaven. If God should put redemption, forgiveness, and salvation on any other basis than that of simple faith. then the entire human race would be shut out. But having put the gift of eternal life on the basis of receiving by believing, the whole human race is included and invited to accept it. Our God is a good God. He has made terms that are available to all and out of the reach of none.

Faith is the same in every language. Anyone of any color may believe. From every corner of the earth there will be those in glory who have believed God. The Italian and the Ethiopian may be united in this common faith. The Frenchman and the German will find their hearts drawn together in this saving belief. The Japanese and the Chinese may sit together at the Lord's table in the enjoyment of this mutual confidence and trust in Jesus Christ. This universal faith makes a universal brotherhood. This universal faith would bring a universal peace, if exercised by all. This universal faith gives us a universal gospel and a universal mission to men. Is this your faith? Believe God today and accept Christ now!

The Miracle of a Universal Preservation

The miracle of a universal preservation may well cause us to stand with bared heads in reverential worship. No other gift in all the world will keep one from perishing. The gift of medicines preserves for a while; the gift of fuel will keep the body warm for a limited time; the gift of money will preserve from poverty, but it may be the means of corruption in honey. This gift from Jesus Christ preserves the whole man. His talents are preserved, and his gifts. His money is spent for worth-while things. His time is given to that which is profitable and useful. His words are good words, bringing glory to God and blessing to men.

This gift of God preserves every man who receives Jesus Christ. The native of Africa puts away his heathen customs and begins a civilized life. The wicked man in America puts away his wickedness and begins to live a godly and useful life. The profane man begins to speak words of kindness and truth. Those whose lives are crushed with wretchedness and sorrow become singing saints, serving as they sing. Those who have spent their money on transient pleasures and on sinful pursuits are now found investing in heavenly treasures, laying up gifts for eternity. How blessed it is to know that the life has not been wasted!

The Miracle of a Universal Blessing

The miracle of a universal blessing brings to our hearts a new hope, a new joy, and a new purpose. How hard and difficult it is to try to live a Christian life when one is not a Christian! How laborious it is to try to be good when the life of the good God and His good Spirit are not within us! What a grind it is to try to lay aside the habits of the week in order to be a good Christian on Sunday! God's plan is not this plan; God's way is not this way.

God has designed an entirely different arrangement, whereby He gives to the soul who trusts Jesus Christ a new life, His own life. It is called in one place "The Divine Nature." There are two ways of keeping a pig out of a mud puddle. Man's way is to surround the mud puddle with ten or more coils of barbed wire, fencing it in with the wires spaced closely together, so that the pig cannot get through them to the mud. God's way is to change the pig into a sheep, so that the new nature which it receives will create a desire to stay out of the mud and to rejoice in the clover patch instead. God is not in the business of training, molding, and improving man's normal nature. He is occupied in giving to men a new nature, which is His own life implanted in the heart of the believer. The gift of this new life is assured to the believer in the verse which we are contemplating. The gift of this life is a miracle. In no other way can enemies be brought together.

CHAPTER II

THE STORY OF REDEMPTION IN JOHN 3:16

EVERY human heart should have a deep interest in this great subject. We have been sold under sin and each one of us should realize it fully. Sin overwhelms and overcomes. Sin wrecks and ruins. Sin conquers and overcomes. Sin is never satiated; it always cries for more. Sin crushes but never heals. Sin is always destructive and never constructive.

The Origin of Redemption

God's sovereign solution for every problem caused by Satan's poison of sin is found in John 3:16–"For God so loved . . . that he gave." No human heart contrived such a scheme. No human brain ever devised such a plan. No laboratory on earth could produce such a marvelous way of redemption, as that which came from God's heart and mind.

It was God who thought of sending His Son. It was His own great knowledge that revealed the helplessness of man and his inability to redeem himself. God and only God found a way whereby a sinner could be changed into a saint, a wicked man-made fit for glory. He not only thought out the plan, but He arranged with His own Son to carry it out.

Christ said, "Now the Lord GOD, and his Spirit, hath sent me" (Isa. 48:16). All the three persons of the Godhead were united in originating this plan for our eternal redemption.

The Object of Redemption

Redemption was provided for the people of the entire world. No lesser number has been included in this great blessing. It is offered freely to all. Redemption was not for the angels, nor for the animals. It was for guilty men who need redemption. None are excluded from this great objective, although there are many who do not want to be included. God's kindness is manifested by His universal offer. Included in this plan are the black, the white, the red, the yellow, and the brown. In this expression may be found the rich and the poor. The sick or the well may come. The strong and the weak are invited. Those who are prominent and those who are obscure are likewise included.

Geographical location makes no difference, for this word includes ALL the world and omits none. The peasant in poverty is included, as well as the prince in the palace. The washerwoman may rejoice that she is one of them, while the king may be glad that he is not omitted.

The Plan of Redemption

God's heart is unveiled and unfolded in this great illumination of John 3:16. Man would have devised quite a different plan. Men have devised various plans of redemption. But the divine plan, as revealed in this passage, is that God gave His Son. **We are redeemed in a very simple way and yet one that is most effectual. God's plan is that Christ should do it all**. God's program makes provision for only one participant, and that one is Jesus Christ, His Son. There is no room in His plan for our pet ideas, nor our peculiar notions. His is a finished plan, needing no additions nor subtractions by us. His plan admits of no failure; it is a successful plan. His plan produces results. Those who are redeemed by Jesus Christ are really saved; they know it and others know it. Their lives reflect the truth of it; their lips acknowledge the reality of it. They are delivered from Satan's oppression and become redeemed men who love their Redeemer.

The Purpose of Redemption

God's objective is revealed in our verse by the words, "should not perish." What a great purpose it is! Those who are redeemed will not perish like the old world, but be saved like Noah. They will not perish like Sodom, but be delivered like Lot. They will not perish like the foolish virgins, but receive a royal welcome as did the wise ones. They will not perish like the rich man, but have a convoy of angels to glory like Lazarus. They will not perish like the devil shall perish but will live eternally with Christ. What a purpose! What a plan! What a program! What a provision! And all of this is wrapped up in Jesus Christ.

Millions are spent on paint to keep the wood from perishing. Millions are spent on medicines to keep the body from perishing. Millions are spent on sprays and chemicals to keep the plants from perishing. Millions are spent on locks to keep our valuables from perishing. Millions are spent on life-insurance to keep the family from perishing, Millions are spent on monuments to prevent the memory from perishing. Millions are spent on dams, revetments, and sea-walls to prevent the land from perishing. Millions are spent on caskets and containers to prevent the corpses from perishing. Millions are spent on life-boats and life preservers to keep the passengers from perishing. Millions are spent on weather-proofing to prevent merchandise from perishing. But God gave Jesus Christ to keep You from perishing. What a purpose God had! May it be fulfilled in You.

The Extent of Redemption

Let us notice how great is the scope of this redemption. Christ used the word "WHOSOEVER." He wanted to include you. He wanted to include children with their parents. He would not exclude the laboring man, nor the captains of industry. He would have the politician know that he, too, is acceptable. The prisoner in the cell may learn that he will have a welcome, if he comes to Christ in his sin. The judge and the criminal are alike included. The queen in her royal splendor, and the pauper in her poverty are both alike welcome under this gracious, all-inclusive word. The religious man may enter his claim here, and so may the ungodly man. Both are invited. Neither the Jew nor the Gentile should feel that he is not wanted with such a word presented to him by the Saviour.

We may go with this word "WHOSOEVER" into the hold of the ship and tell the stoker that he is included, or we may go to the bridge of the ship and tell the captain, too. By this we are emboldened to approach the school teacher, or give the same message to the scholar at the desk. This invitation extends to the president of the brewery and also to the poor, deluded man who drinks its product. By this we are authorized to take the precious gospel to the president of the bank, or to visit the janitor as he sits down in the furnace room waiting to sweep the floors. The architect, the engineer, the brick-mason, the sign painter, the blacksmith, the auto mechanic, the mother and her daughter, the father and his son, all are alike taken into this magnificent word "WHOSOEVER."

The Application of Redemption

This is a joyful meditation, for it applies to all who "BELIEVE ON HIM." Christ is clearly presented as the object of faith. Redemption is only for those who have a saving interest in Jesus Christ. Since He is the Redeemer, all must come to Him. You must come to Him, if redemption is to be yours. He redeems those who need to be redeemed and realize it. Although His redemption is for the "whosoevers," it is obtained only by those who are the "whosoever_wills." God shuts out all the "whosoever_won'ts." His redemption is free, but It must be taken as a gift. As medicine is only effective when it is applied to the wound, so redemption is only effective when it is applied to the soul.

This redemption is not for religious observance, nor can it be purchased with money, nor is it obtained because of prayers or tears. It is God's gift to the believer. It is God's blessing for the one who trusts Jesus Christ. It is God's benefaction for the one who places his case in the hands of Christ, the Redeemer. You should let Him be your Redeemer. Believe that He *can*, the He *will*, and that

He *does* redeem you. Kneel at His feet just now, and let Him redeem YOU.

The Result of Redemption

We should be deeply interested in the effects of redemption. Those who are redeemed will never perish. They will have everlasting life. Life prevents decay. There is no corruption where there is life. Dead bodies need to be preserved, but not living bodies. Those who are redeemed are preserved in their entirety.

It is true that the soul will not perish, but it is also true that the life will not perish. The voice of the redeemed is used for God's glory. The money is invested in God's business. The talents are placed at the disposal of the Redeemer. The efforts are spent for the glory of God. The time is occupied in His service. The whole of the redeemed man is saved from perishing. The entire life becomes valuable to God and useful to men. The results of his labor become imperishable. Has He redeemed You? Make Him yours today!

CHAPTER III

THE GREAT THINGS OF JOHN 3:16

WHEN the angel said, "He shall be great" (Luke 1:32), he made a statement which has no measurements. The greatness of Christ Jesus is seen in His power to create, the variety of His creations, His power to transform human lives, and His marvelous revelation of the Father. In this chapter there are presented some of the great things of God spoken from the lips of this great Son of God.

In this beautiful statement of our Lord will be found twelve of the greatest truths for the human heart:

The Greatest Lover

This lovely One is brought to our attention in the opening statement, "For GOD." Love is found in every nationality. Love appeals to every human heart. Love has affected every life. The presence of it brings a sweet joy and peace. The absence of it brings sorrow, grief, war, pain, and utmost anguish.

History records the story of great love affairs. The record of Napoleon and his love experiences is a story of intrigue, disappointment, and sorrow. Shakespeare took advantage of love affairs to illustrate, in graphic manner, the experiences of human hearts, and some of his statements and characters have become known throughout the world.

Here God is presented to us as the greatest Lover. He has loved us; He has loved His enemies; He has loved the unlovely. He has loved those who have forfeited all right to His love. He has loved sinners who loved their sins. He has loved even those who would dethrone Him and crush Him if they could. His love has continued through sickness and health, through poverty and wealth, through shadow and sunshine. His love continues from the cradle to the grave. His heart is great enough to include all and to include them at all times. What a wonderful Lover He is! No one can question His love, nor doubt it after having a look at Calvary.

The Greatest Degree

Of course, He speaks of love. The love of God is measured by Calvary. Love is always measured by the gift or the sacrifice which it makes. Princely love is accompanied by princely gifts. Love among paupers is accompanied by the poorest of gifts. A gift is measured, of course, by the ability of the giver. God has proved His love for you by giving to you the most marvelous gift that could ever be conceived by either heart or mind–the gift of His own Son, the maker of heaven and earth. Sometimes there has been given as a love-gift a kingdom with a crown and a scepter. Not always has this gift been a blessing, sometimes it has brought endless trouble. Others have given gifts of great sums of money. This wealth has not always been a blessing, sometimes it has brought sorrow of heart, and has been a curse. God gave His Son, gave Him to You. This gift will lift the load from the heart, drive the tears from the eyes, remove the robe of ashes and replace it with the garment of gladness. This gift will cause the mourning to cease and the singing to begin. He who accepts this gift of Jesus Christ is saved and safe and satisfied. He can sing and rejoice alway. No other gift compares with this in value. No other gift is so precious. No other gift produces such marvelous results.

The Greatest Company

"THE WORLD" is included in the message of this passage and none are excluded. All are the subjects of His love and none are overlooked. All other lovers have a very restricted love. The king loves his own subjects, not those of neighboring countries. The doctor cares for his own patients, not those of another doctor. The father loves his own children, not the children of the neighborhood. All love is circumscribed and includes only a few, but the love of God described by Christ in this verse is all inclusive and embraces every human heart that loves.

It is quite like God to do this. He sends the rain "on the just and on the unjust." He causes His sun to shine on the righteous and on the wicked. He causes the blessings of earth to fall upon the godly and upon the ungodly as well. In the same way He has loved and given in such a way as to embrace every heart of every race and in every class of society. He has forgotten none in His expanse of love, He has included you, no matter who you are, nor where you are, nor what you are. Satan may have urged you to believe that you have been forsaken and forgotten by God, but such is not the case. Our Lord Jesus Christ has said specifically that you are included because you are a part of the world. Do believe in His love! Do let Him love you !

The Greatest Act

There is no greater act in all the world than that described in these words in John 3: 16–"THAT HE GAVE." Our histories are filled with the great acts of men. Some have fought mighty battles and won marvelous victories. Others have accomplished great feats in exploration. There are those who have brought about beneficent changes in the treatment of human ills and ailments, and to these we owe a debt of gratitude. Wonderful engineering feats have been accomplished and transportation problems have been solved by human endeavors. But none of these acts are the greatest acts. None of these affect the human soul. none transform a sinful life.

The greatest act of all is the giving on the part of God of His Son to sinning and sinful men. He has given Christ to You. There is no question about it, but possibly you have not accepted that gift, nor received by faith that wonderful Son as your own. It is the taking of the gift that accomplishes the culmination of the transaction. The offering of the gift is not enough. You must take the gift and make this lovely One your own. Other gifts have been given to you and you have accepted them; they have been worn out and discarded. Here is a gift which by the greatest act is sent to your heart for acceptance. Do thank God that He ever performed this marvelous miracle on your behalf !

The Greatest Gift

John 3 :16 brings the greatest of all gifts to our attention. This gift is priceless. All other gifts bear a price. This gift cannot be purchased with money. Other gifts may. This gift never fades, nor decays, nor diminishes. Other gifts corrode, wear out, become useless and worthless, finally to be discarded. This gift enriches the recipient forever. Other gifts are temporary in their blessing. This gift brings an abundance of joy and adds no sorrow with it. Other gifts may bring a heartbreak and a heartache.

This gift is the only gift in all the world which may be taken to the gates of the tomb, through the dark valley, and out into the blessed sunlight of God's presence. Other gifts must be left behind for others to enjoy. This gift does not change with changing years. Other gifts get out of date, out of style, and must be laid away. Where was there ever a gift like this? The longer you have this gift the more precious does this treasure become to the soul.

The Greatest Opportunity

Our Lord and Saviour, Jesus Christ, made the greatest offer of all time in the words of our text— "THAT WHOSOEVER." This is all-bracing and all-inclusive. It is told to every man, woman, and child. It presents to every human heart the opportunity and privilege to become a child of God, an heir of glory, and a citizen of heaven. Other opportunities are for those who have money, or position, or education. This opportunity embraces all and each, and every individual, regardless of his talents or native ability. Here is an opportunity which is universal in its character and world-wide in its application. This privilege is offered to men and women of every nation, every language and in every place.

"WHOSOEVER" is the greatest word that could be used in God's call to men. It includes all and omits none. This world-wide word was used by Christ in order that your own individual heart might be encouraged to believe that this gift of Christ was for you. What a lovely response there should be from your heart! Thank God that you may have Christ and that you may now take Christ. God grant that you will!

The Greatest Simplicity

This simplicity is found in the word "BELIEVETH." No more simple thing can be found in all human, mental processes than this. To believe God is the acme of simplicity and ease. And yet it is one of the greatest forces of life. It is the great common habit of life. We sit upon a chair, because we believe in it. We place ourselves at the disposal of the dentist, because we believe in him. We buy bread and eat it, because we believe it is good food for the body. We drop a letter in the box, for we believe in the postal system. We consult the time-table of the railroad, for we believe it is truthful. We live by believing.

God has asked us, through Christ Jesus, to believe His Word. Why should we not believe Him? Christ said, "If I tell you the truth, why do you not believe me?"

Believing is automatic when the mind is convinced of the facts. If any who read these lines is doubting God, then I pray you to begin to believe God and to believe in His Son, Jesus Christ.

The Greatest Attraction

There is nothing so attractive to our hearts and minds as these words, "IN HIM." Many things are brought before us to attract our love and faith. Music entrances some, schemes attract others, politics appeal to many hearts, and the pursuit of pleasure allures others. The military has a strong appeal to a few, and educational processes entice the hearts of many. But none of these are held out by our Lord Jesus as the greatest attraction in the world. Christ Jesus Himself is the One.

God would have us allured, attracted and enticed by this lovely person, Jesus Christ, the Saviour of men. Jesus said, "And I, if I be lifted up from the earth, will draw all men unto me." There is none so fair as He.

Others may be beautiful, but He is "altogether lovely." Others may have power, but He is higher than the highest. He should attract our love and faith and trust to His own blessed person.

The Greatest Promise

There is no promise so great as this blessed assurance, "SHOULD NOT PERISH." Everything around us perishes; shoes, automobiles, ships, houses, hats, human bodies, all perish. But here is the greatest promise of all, that the person who makes Jesus Christ his own will never perish. His soul will not perish and neither will his body; neither will his talents, nor his influence. God saves the whole man when that man wholly trusts Jesus Christ.

The Greatest Difference

The mightiest change in all human experience is wrapped up in that little word "BUT." This word is a division line between the saved and the lost, between the righteous and the unrighteous, between the godly and the ungodly, between the forgiven and the unforgiven, between the justified and the guilty, between those who live in Christ, and those who are dead in their sins. What a difference!

The believer will not die but live. He will not perish but be saved. He will not dwell in the dark but in the light. He will not be shut out but he will enter in. He will not be afar off but made nigh. He will not sigh but will sing. He will not be punished but will be blessed. The "but" makes all the difference!

The Greatest Certainty

Utmost assurance is necessary in such a vital and important matter as the salvation of the soul. Our Lord gives us this certainty in the word "HAVE." There need be no question on the part of the sinner as to his salvation when Christ Jesus is trusted, for "HAVE" certainly is definite and clear and positive, admitting of no misinterpretation nor mis-understanding. To have Christ is to have life. To trust the soul to Jesus Christ results in the possession of the blessed gift of life, which links one eternally with the living God. "HAVE" does not mean Hope. "HAVE" does not mean SUPPOSE. "HAVE" does not mean PERHAPS.

There can be no question about the word "HAVE." Either you HAVE life, or you do not HAVE it. Either you HAVE Christ because you received Him by faith, or you do not HAVE Him. The acceptance of Christ brings the gift of eternal life and salvation. You may have the peace and the joy of knowing that you HAVE Him when, by faith, you kneel to HIM and accept HIM for your own.

The Greatest Possession

That priceless gift, the greatest and best of all possible gifts of life, is described by these two words, "EVERLASTING LIFE." No gift can be compared with this. No possession should be so much loved, prized, or valued, as the eternal life of the eternal God. How blessedly true it is that the one who has this life within his bosom is eternally linked with the eternal God who gave it!

This life enables the receiver to live like its Author in some degree. This life is a new life. It is resurrection, incorruptible life. It is a life that sin and death cannot touch. It is not a product of any human efficiency. It comes down from above. This life does not grow in any earthly garden, it is a plant of heavenly growth, and it makes those who have it a heavenly people. What a great loss to be without it! To possess it is a sure token of eternal joy and bliss ; to be without it is to be assured of spending eternity in outer darkness with none of the blessings of God to be enjoyed or experienced.

CHAPTER IV

SOME MARVELS IN THIS SUPERIOR VERSE

THE followers of Jesus Christ should be prepared to see and hear wonderful things. The unusual pervades the Christian life. "Great and marvelous are thy works" (Rev. 15:3). Some of these marvels are found in the verse which we are considering. We may expect that a Saviour who is so wonderful should utter marvelous statements for our ediflcation. Let us consider them.

The Greatest Word

This word is found in this passage and tells us of the most wonderful Person in all the world. The word "GOD" immediately calls our attention to One who is incomprehensible and yet He invites us to know Him. We are urged to draw near to this great Person who is unapproachable. We are given the privilege of listening to One whose voice will shake the earth and whose message is eternal. We have brought before us, immediately, a Person who is greater than all the great things that He has created and made.

What a great word is this little word, GOD! it is a word that attracts the attention of the natives of every nation, the citizens of every city. This is the One who was from the past eternity and shall continue throughout the coming eternity. The greatest efforts in the world are connected with Him; the greatest power in the universe issues from His fiat. This great Name calls for a great faith and demands a great trust. This great Person calls for an ultra-loyal service. This great Word will make those great who learn to know Him, love Him, and trust Him.

The Sweetest Word

The sweetest word in human language is here. It is the word "LOVE." What is more alluring to the heart, or more attractive to the mind, or more interesting to the soul than this precious little word, "LOVE!" It is the heritage of every heart. The black man loves, the yellow man loves, the red man loves, the white man loves, the brown man loves–they all love. Love affairs are found among every people, and love is transferred from heart to heart in every language.

This sweet word stills the hearts of mothers and babies, as they love in that sweet, tender way which cannot be imitated nor simulated. What a romance there is in the love of lovers! What deeds of valor have been wrought to bring lovers together! What risks have been permitted and invited! Love will not be denied. Love finds a way. Love will lead the lover through the fire and the flame, through the flood and the forest, through the trackless jungles and over the stormy sea. Love will brook no interference; love must have the object of its affections. How sweet this word is!

Love expressed is the supreme accomplishment of the human heart. Here is a love between the lovely God and an unlovely sinner; between a holy God and an unholy sinner; between a good God and a bad sinner. Here is love from God to you , my friend. It is God's sweetest gift for you.

The Broadest Word

The word of greatest scope to the mind is found in that word, "WORLD." it is so broad that none are omitted and not one is excluded. It is so wide that all are included and none are excepted. It includes even You, whoever you may be. In the world there is a marvelous and wonderful variety of human beings. There are the pigmies who were originally Hindus or natives of India. What a strange, peculiar class of people they arel They travel here and there without a home! And there is no attraction among them, and yet God loves them

There are the Polynesians who live in the South Sea Islands. They live such a strange, unusual life, cutting their bodies, worshipping idols, deforming their heads, yet God loves them. The wild bushmen of South Africa, who are so short in stature, have such a peculiar color, and wear their hair in such strange fashions, but these, too, are a part of that great world loved by God. Then there are the Hottentots, Fijians, the Papuans, the Bedouins, and the Eskimos. How many strange people there are whom we would never love, but God's love is of such a broad and inclusive nature that it includes all of these.

It includes the drunkard, the harlot, the thief, the murderer, the robber. His love includes You, with an your sins and deficiencies and faults. How broad this wonderful love is!

The Greatest Kindness

The sweetest way to express this grace is by the word "GAVE." Cruel men are grasping men. They want things for themselves. Cruel monarchs wreck nations to obtain what they desire for themselves. Great countries overwhelm the smaller ones in their search for more land and more wealth. Wicked men will torture the wealthy to obtain their jewelry and their gold. Great corporations will strangle and starve the weak and small competitors, that they may obtain all the business. God is kind, God gave, God gives and keeps on giving. When choice was to be made between Christ, the great Giver, and Barabbas, the great robber, the people chose Barabbas, and the Holy Spirit of God immediately wrote, "Now Barabbas was a robber" (John 18:40) .

God is a great giver. Those who have the life of God within their own hearts by saving faith in Christ Jesus have also become great givers. God is always giving. He gives life and health and breath to all. He gives the sunshine and the rain, He gives the harvest's golden grain. He gives without considering the character of the recipient. He gives without waiting to be asked, nor expecting to be thanked. He gives through the long years of life, and gives without measure or restraint. How kind God is! There is none so kind as He.

Others are kind if a return will be made to them. Some are kind only to those who are grateful, and are kind to those who can pay them back with interest. Much kindness is based on selfishness. God's kindness comes from a heart that is wonderfully gracious and is not waiting for results. He is kind to the good and to the bad; to the wicked and to the righteous; to the rich and to the poor.

The Most Comprehensive Word

The most all-embracing word in our language is found in John 3:16. It is the word "WHOSOEVER." Every human heart should rejoice at the sound of this word. There are those who are victims of circumstances, who have been crushed to the ground in their efforts to ascend, who have been hurt and harmed by the cruelty and perfidy of friends, but each of these may find a refuge in this precious word "WHOSOEVER."

There are those who are miserable in their riches, they are included. There are those who are content to live in squalor and poverty, this word includes them also. The fireman in the hold of the ocean liner is mentioned in this word, and so is the president of the state university. The master and the servant are comprehended together in this statement. The sovereign and the slave are brought together in this all comprehensive and all-encircling word. The general in the army and the private who carries the gun are alike included. The king on his throne, together with the peasant in the field, may both rejoice in having a portion in this verse. The surgeon who is operating and the patient lying on the table, together with the nurse in her white apparel, all may take refuge under this lovely word. The teacher behind the desk, and the pupil sitting before her in the room, together with the janitor of the building and the architect who built it, may all find a resting place in this all-embracing word, "WHOSOEVER."

The Most Decisive Word

The word "NOT" is both certain and sure. This word leaves no shadow of doubt. There is no question about it. It is beyond dispute. It cannot be contested, nor questioned. This word cannot admit of two interpretations. It is unending. Its fiat is infallible, it is a word that can be depended upon. That soul who believes in Jesus Christ shall "NOT" perish.

There is no possibility of misinterpreting this statement. It is conclusive and final. It needs no commentary to express it; it needs no authority to unfold it; it needs no interpreter to translate it; it means that the soul that belongs to Jesus Christ is saved and safe. How decisive is this little word "NOT!" What rest it brings to the mind! All questioning is at an end when we read the word. "NOT." We need have no more anxious thoughts. We can rest surely upon this irrefutable and undeniable word.

When God says "NOT," we should thank Him for that little word. It does lift our feet from the miry clay to set them upon a rock. It quickly drives all of our doubts to the dungeon. It immediately dispels all the shadows of unbelief, and fills the soul with a radiance of faith. It is God who said that word "NOT;" it is for us to believe it with rejoicing.

The Most Tragic Word

What hopeless sorrow is expressed by the word "perish"! We think of the ocean liner pounding to pieces upon the rocky shore of the desolate land. We think of the strong swimmer caught in the current and carried over the falls. We think of the miner down under the falling slate and crushed to death. We think of the wonderful palace torn by the hurricane, and twisted to bits and finally destroyed. We think of the great city damaged by an earthquake, and left a pile of wreckage and ruins. But here it is the soul that is under consideration.

The destruction of the works of men's hands is not nearly so serious as the wreck and ruin of a human life. It is surely heart-breaking to gaze upon those who have permitted sin to destroy both the body and the soul, and bring to naught the great ambitions of life.

Man should be like a beautiful garden, fllled with fragrant and delightful flowers, but instead of that, his life is overgrown with weeds and tangled vines. Man's life should be like a harp with well-tuned strings, giving forth harmonious melodies to refresh other lives, but instead of that, the strings are broken and only discordant sounds are heard when it is touched. His manhood has decayed, his ambitions have failed, his plans have been wrecked, and over his whole life is written that awful word, "Perished." Only Christ can save man from perishing!

The Most Certain Word

The word "HAVE" is not ambiguous. Our Lord used this word so that there should be no question about the instantaneous power of eternal life in our hearts when we really trusted in Jesus Christ. This word assures us of the possession of that priceless gift which comes only from heaven. We possess and enjoy this blessing of eternal life now. It is not a question of eternal life being loaned to us, nor is the gift of life predicated upon certain acts on our part.

This word assures us that we HAVE it. It is in our hearts. It is in our possession. It is in our hands. It is within our souls. We have a firm hold on it and it has a firm hold on us. We belong to it and it belongs to us. God vested us with eternal life. By faith we live in the enjoyment of it. Eternal life is in our stock; it is in our store; it is a very part of ourselves. How certain is the sound of this short word! Let us praise God for it. Let us love Christ for it. Let us believe the Holy Spirit about it. Let us rejoice in the blessing of it. We HAVE it, because we HAVE HIM.

The Most Mysterious Word

There is not a more mysterious word than "LIFE." Life puzzles the greatest and the best of men. No one understands it, or knows what it is. No one knows how it starts, nor why it ceases, nor of what it consists. Life has always been the subject of human investigation. But the laboratory gives no answer. The grave mocks at man's inquiry. Only God knows what it is. Only God can give life. Only God can direct life. Only God can dispose of life. And the life referred to in John 3: 16 is the life of God.

The great fact of the implanting of that life in the human heart is manifested when that heart trusts the Lord Jesus Christ. Every animal has a life which was given to it by God. It has a life of its own, and it lives its own life. The dog does not live like the deer; the cat does not live like the cow: the chicken does not live like the pig; neither does one plant live like an other plant. The wheat will not grow like the apple tree, nor will the lettuce climb like the honeysuckle. The gourd will not produce like a grape vine. Each plant lives its own life.

But in John 3: 16 is revealed a new life which only God can give, and He calls it eternal or everlasting life. It is the very nature of God implanted in a human heart. Only God can give it to man. God grant that you will receive it now and receive it more abundantly. The life that enjoys God must come *from* God. The life that agrees with God must be the product of God. This life is free and may be received from God by a simple faith in Jesus Christ, the Lord and Saviour.

CHAPTER V

SIX WONDERS OF THE VERSE

THE wonders of nature attract both the old and young . None become so educated that they cease to be amazed and astounded at many of the wonders in the world around us. This verse is full of wonders and we shall consider six of them in the present chapter.

The Wonder of Its Author

We are led to stand in amazement as we realize that the great truths of this verse came from the heart of God. No one else would have conceived such a salvation. No mind on earth could have devised such a plan, nor have provided such a way for sinful men. Its source being in God assures us of its purity and its sufficiency. Since we are traveling to eternity, it is most assuring to realize that our sojourn here has been arranged for by a loving and an almighty God.

This salvation described in John 3:16 is as great as its author. God would not think of an imperfect thing, nor provide an insufficient thing; for as He is perfect, so is His work perfect. It is God who gave us Christ; it is God who loved; it is God who saves the believer.

The Wonder of Its Object

The purpose revealed here surely attracts our hearts to God. He "loved the world." Pause for a moment and think of the millions and millions of people that inhabit our earth, people in all walks of life, some civilized and some uncivilized, some rich and some poor. Every kind both in age and condition is included.

There are those with horrid dispositions, cruel men and women, harmful and hurtful in all their dealings. Some are selfish and self-seeking, they override and overrule everything that is contrary to their own will and wish, in order that they may obtain their own way.

Then there are also those who are kind, gracious, and lovable, and these it would be easy to love. Such was the rich young ruler concerning whom it was said, "Jesus beholding him loved him."

There are heathen who live terrible lives ; their bodies are vile, their habits and ways are most repugnant, their customs are cruel, and yet they, too, are the objects of God's love and care.

There are some who are very antagonistic to God. They hate Him and with a heart full of animosity and antagonism they defy Him and deny Him. But God's wonderful love extends even to these.

If you will think of those whom you like the least and despise the most, you will find that they, too, are the objects of God's grace and are included in His wonderful offer of salvation.

The Wonder of the Recipient

This great trust is an amazing revelation to our hearts. You may be that fortunate one. You may become the most blessed person in all the world, because the offer is for whosoever–wheresoever you may be, or whatsoever you may be. The recipient may be a little child or an aged grandmother. He may be a college professor, or a railroad engineer, or a stenographer. The recipient is that one who receives this wonderful salvation from such a wonderful God in such a wonderfully simple way.

No qualifications are necessary at all, except that you feel your need of Him and will accept the gift. There are no financial requirements and no educational demands. If you have ears to hear the call, you may receive Christ. If you have a heart that feels its need, you may receive this salvation. If you are old enough to understand that God loves you and has given Christ to you, then you may be this recipient and enjoy the blessings of this wonderful verse of Scripture.

The Wonder of the Son

This magnificent truth is enough to fill and thrill our souls with ecstasy and rapture. The One described in this verse as "The only begotten Son" is the only Son of His Father. He is the only Heir of His Father. He is the One who made the worlds. "All things were made by him, and for him." The wool, the silk, and the cotton that you wear, and all the food that you eat were made by and for the Lord Jesus Christ. You and I simply have it by His grace and enjoy it because He is willing to bestow it. We live constantly by the good grace of God.

Why Christ should care for us is a mystery! Why God should send His Son to Calvary that He might bring us to Glory we cannot understand! He said "Farewell" to His Son in Heaven, in order that He might say "Welcome" to us on earth. He handed over His Son to cruel men and permitted them to accomplish their will on Him and against Him, in order that He might use that very sacrifice for our salvation. The Saviour who was treated so cruelly by wicked men is the very One who calls so lovingly for the unrighteous to come to Him and be saved.

The Son of God was not an ordinary man; He was and is the God-man. He made the worlds by the word of His mouth, and yet He has time for you and me. He has almighty power and can make anything that He wants, any time that He wishes, yet His tender bosom makes room for the weary and the heavy laden. Christ will work wonders in your life with His wonder-working power. Think for a moment of the honor of having Him as your own Lord and Saviour, your Companion for eternity. Surely you will want to accept this wonderful and wonder-working Saviour just now so that you may belong to Him !

The Wonder of the Offer

God's great liberality should cause us to bow our heads in reverence and worship. The offer is made to the "whosoevers" who believe. God holds out no blessing for the one who doubts. God has nothing to give to the one who argues with Him. He has no blessings for those who disagree with Him. Believers are the only ones who receive God's salvation. The one who believes God has all the resources of heaven at his command. This offer includes all who believe and omits none; it embraces each person in all the world between the cradle and the grave, and includes you in that circle. Since Christ has used the word "whosoever," what an opportunity it offers for you to step into that circle of favor and say, "Thank you, my Lord, I believe You, I believe on Jesus Christ, I accept your gift."

God is not offering to sell this great blessing to you, nor does heaven suggest that it will be a prize for the one who wins the race. This offer is a gift, a priceless present; it is a donation to the believing soul from the great heart of the living God. He is offering to give you a Person, not an experience. He is offering you His Son, not simply forgiveness, peace, and pardon. He offers you the One who is the Chief among ten thousand and altogether lovely. He gives to you for your own personal possession that One whom angels worship and before whom the seraphim cover their faces with their wings. This offer is a limited offer; it is only for believers in its scope, and only in this life as to its time element. The offer must be accepted now. None can be saved in eternity.

Christ is not offered to those who are in hell. Who have passed the judgment bar and been consigned to the eternal penitentiary. "The Son of man hath power on earth to forgive sins." it is here and now that the offer is made, and one of its conditions is that it must be accepted here and now. The offer is to give you Christ that He may save you in this present life, be your Saviour when death's shadows fall athwart your path and preserve you to and through His eternal kingdom.

The Wonder of the Blessings

The many beatitudes which are revealed in this passage causes us to rejoice in the great goodness of God. Two blessings are proffered us. One is negative, "should not perish"; the other is positive, "have everlasting life." Surely no one wishes to perish. Everything else perishes and decays. All around us are the evidences of these changes. The trees rot at the heart and are blown over by the wind; stones soften with age and are washed by the rains; buildings decay and fall; animals and birds die; great institutions are filled with the wrecked bodies of human beings. We are constantly faced with the fact that every created thing perishes and decays.

Here is a blessing offered to the believing soul, a blessing that we should grasp quickly and praise God for eternally. Think of having the whole life preserved forever. Think of the joy of knowing that your daily life is to be safe forever in God. Think of being so profitable to God that He preserves what you do and say unto His heavenly kingdom. What a wonder it is that we may live a life which never ends and speak words which shall continue to speak forever! The gift that He gives is eternal LIFE. It is a new life with all the complications, ramifications, and associations that a life should have.

The sinner out of Christ, with no Saviour and no God, with no Lord to rule His life, lives a human life which is conflned to this earth. He soon dies and his memory is blotted out. We pass the old cemetery where he is buried and see the tombstone toppled over and surrounded by grass and weeds.

Nobody cares for him; his life has been a vapor which appeared for a little while and then vanished away.

But the Christian's life is not a mist but a monument. He is compared to a living stone; he is one who does not crumble with the passing of time, nor perish in the storms of life. He will never perish. His life is preserved and he is preserved. His words and his deeds are alike kept for the Master and recorded in the eternal books of glory.

The Wonder of the Assurance

This blessed assurance brings sweetest peace to the heart of every believer. We may be assured of the certainty of this great salvation, because the Lord Jesus Himself spoke these words. God's Son would not deceive us. Christ would not hold out to us an offer which He could not or would not fulfill. The Lord Jesus would not tantalize us by displaying to our eyes this marvelous blessing of eternal salvation and then keep it just beyond our reach.

I have seen a mule with a pole tied along its back and projecting beyond its nose about eighteen inches; on the end of the pole was suspended an ear of corn just out of the reach of his mouth. The mule kept walking forward and stretching out its neck in its effort to reach this ear of corn, but of course the corn moved as fast as he moved and he never could catch up with it.

Some seem to think that the Saviour is treating them like this with His salvation. Of course, this is not true. The verse assures us that those who believe in Christ HAVE salvation, HAVE eternal life, HAVE eternal deliverance from perishing. How deeply your heart should be stirred by the fact that you may have, here and now, within your heart this life of Jesus, this wonderful gift of God which not only makes you a Christian but enables you day by day to live like a Christian! God grant that you may receive Him now.

JOHN THREE SIXTEEN REFUTES ERRORS

IN the few words of this verse, the Lord Jesus clears away all questions concerning the doctrines of false cults. He shows clearly that these cults are utterly false, and He repudiates in unmistakable language the teachings which they propound. What a magnificent attack the Lord Jesus makes here upon all of His enemies in these satanic religions! Let us briefly consider their claims:

Atheism

The atheist affirms that there is no God. He denies the existence of a Creator and declares that there is no Supreme Person whatever.

But this verse assures us that there is a God, that He has a personal interest in us, and that He is actively engaged in our affairs.

Agnosticism

The agnostic friend hastens to inform us that he does not know anything about God. He is not sure that there is one, though he would not deny that there is a God. He admits that he is ignorant of such a Person, and affirms that all others are as ignorant as himself .

This verse refutes such a statement by declaring quite clearly that there is a God who loves and a God who gave. Thus there are two things that are revealed about God in this one passage which the agnostic denies.

Deism

The followers of this faith would have us believe that if there is a God, He does not care for us, He has no interest in our affairs whatever, but has left the world to pursue its own path and to work out its own complex problems to the best of its ability. But this verse reveals to us that God does care, for He loves, He gave, He saves.

Pantheism

The followers of this peculiar belief would have us find God in nature. They are nature worshippers and would have us look for God in violets, sunsets, mountains, trees, and birds.

This doctrine is also refuted by our wonderful verse, for here we read that God loved "the world," by which we see that God is one Person and the world is something different–the work of His hands and the object of His love and care. No man is in the article which he makes. It may bear his name and may reveal his wonderful mind and the skill of his hands, but the man himself is not in that which he produces. God made all the things of nature, but He Himself is on the throne.

Eddyism

The doctrines of Mrs. Eddy, know as "Christian Science," assert that God is not an individual, a personality, whom we shall see with our eyes when we enter eternity, but rather that He is a state of mind, a thought, an idea, a condition brought about by thinking.

But John 3:16 affirms very clearly that God had a Son, and thoughts have no son. Ideas and conditions cannot give the God-Man, Jesus, who became Lord and Christ.

Unitarianism

These friends teach that there is a God who is a Supreme Being, but deny that Jesus is the Son of God, equal with the Father, and also deny that the Holy Spirit is an individual, a person, who is co-equal with the Father and with the Son.

This declaration of Christ in John 3: 16 reveals that God does have a Son, and that Jesus is the only Son–there is not another. Being God's Son, He must partake of the identical essence and substance of the eternal God on the throne. Rev. Edward Henry Bickersteth, Bishop of Exeter, England, has written a superb and marvelous exposition of this truth in his book, *"The Rock of Ages,"* a book dedicated to the Unitarians of England. (The Francis Emory Fitch Co., New York City.)

Naturalism

There are those who affirm that a Saviour is not needed in the human life. They assure us that it is only necessary to cultivate the natural talents and native goodness found in the human heart and then a Christian life will result. This also is refuted in our verse by the statement that eternal life is a gift from God to the one who believes in Jesus Christ, hence it is not received through education but only by faith.

Legalism

Some well-meaning friends have resurrected the Jewish law as a means of salvation for the believer in the present day. They would have us assume the position of the Jews and, by observing the legalities of the Old Testament, obtain the gift of eternal life.

This error is refuted by the plain statement, "He that believeth on the Son." From this we learn that Christ Jesus is the Saviour, not a system of law-keeping.

Sentimentalism

Some friends have a very tender heart and cannot bear the thought of salvation through the shed blood of Christ. They call our gospel "The Bloody Theory of the Atonement."

In the passage we are considering, we read "God gave." He gave Him to Calvary, He gave Him over to His enemies, He gave Him over to the cruel cross, He gave Him to die. The fish dies for the one who eats it, the sheep dies for those who feed on mutton, the cow dies that the hungry may have food. All vegetables die that, through their death, we who eat them may have life. Death resulting in life is the universal rule of all kingdoms.

Ecclesiasticism

Throughout the ages, religion has been in constant conflict with the gospel of the Saviour. Membership in some religious organization, and the acceptance of certain religious doctrines and dogmas, have been presented to the public as a means of salvation and a method of receiving forgiveness of sins. Our verse clearly assures us that eternal life is received only by those who believe in Jesus Christ. Since it is by believing in Him, Ecclesiasticism is automatically excluded as a means or method of salvation.

Judaism

Class or group salvation is another error which is refuted by our verse. Some would say, "If you belong to us, you are all right for eternity. All others are lost." There are many groups who make this affirmation, and there are thousands who believe it.

The error of this assertion is clearly evidenced by that precious word, "Whosoever." Hereby all are included, and none are excluded. Here every weary heart may find a welcome.

Universalism

This strange theory, or hypothesis, would have us believe that everybody is a child of God and that all will be saved. They inform us that the Christian and the cannibal will eventually occupy the same home with God in glory. The godless drunkard and the godly deacon will eventually be reunited in one sweet fellowship in the holy of holies. This fallacious doctrine is denied in the expression, "Whosoever believeth," which limits salvation to the believer. And it is also refuted by telling us that the believer will not perish, which clearly indicates that the unbeliever will perish.

Modernism

The teaching of a social gospel is called "Modernism." it purports to offer a means and method of upbuilding the human race by culture, by refining influences, by building clean homes to take the place of tenements, by paying higher wages, and by eating better food.

This false teaching is utterly denied by our verse which says that God gave His Son that we might receive a new life. The old life will not do, even though it be polished, refined, educated, cultivated, and made religious.

Annihilationism

Those who hold this doctrine teach that the wicked will be blotted out of existence. Some affirm that all, both good and bad, die like the ox or the dog, and have no existence whatever after death. Nowhere in the Bible do we read of the soul being blotted out, or obliterated, or annihilated. Christ used the word "perish" in our verse.

Nowhere does this word ever indicate that the thing which perishes has ceased to exist. If an examination is made of each place where the word occurs, it will be readily seen that our Lord is only speaking of the destruction of the thing for the purpose for which it was intended. "Thy money perish with thee" (Acts 8:20) certainly did not indicate that the money was to cease to exist. "The bottles shall perish" (Luke 5:37) could not mean that the bottles ceased to exist, but having burst they were not fit for further use.

Materialism

The theory is widely promulgated that man has no soul, that the body is all that exists. It is quite certain from our verse that it is the soul which receives eternal life, for the cemetery constantly presents us with the unanswerable fact that the body dies. The Scriptures affirm that there is a body, a soul, and a spirit.

CHAPTER VII

EIGHT REVELATIONS OF GOD

OUR hearts should revel in the blessed fact that God has revealed Himself to Men. He could have kept Himself hidden from us if He had so desired, and we would have had no way of finding Him out. Here in the verse before us, the Lord Jesus reveals God in eight blessed manifestations. Considering the verse carefully, we may have the assurance that we do know God, and that we know His Son in some measure.

Christ Reveals That God "Is"

The atheist says that there is no God, but Christ affirms that there is. The infidel tells us that he does not believe in God, but Christ Jesus advertises that He knows there is a God. Nature in all of its gorgeous glory and remarkable variety reveals to us that there is a God who creates. Of course this lesson is learned from nature by deduction, but Christ gives us this revelation by direct word from His blessed lips. We are not left alone to deductions nor reasons. Since the Lord Jesus Christ could ask, "Which of you convinceth me of sin?" and none responded nor made the attempt, He can also ask, "And if I say the truth, why do you not believe me?"

Since Christ was absolutely true and accurate in every statement which He made, we may believe with the heart that there is a God and that He is the living God who loves and cares. "He that cometh to God must believe that he is" (Heb. 11:6). The way must seem very dark to the one who has no God. The things of life must be strangely mysterious to one who denies the existence of that blessed Person who "worketh all things according to the counsel of his own will." The case must seem desperately hopeless when there is no God in whom to trust.

Christ Reveals God's Interest

God is interested in the welfare of men according to John 3:16. The deist, however, teaches that God is not interested in men, that He does not care and is not concerned with the affairs of men. Christ tells us here that He is interested, for the word "So" certainly expresses to us a tremendous earnestness. a marvelous care, a longing, loving thought toward the children of men.

That word "So" assures us that this great God, who is the living God, does care and cares very deeply for every individual. His care for the body is quite evident, for He has given to men so freely of the greatest variety of foods. There are vegetables of many kinds and fruits of many flavors. There are fabrics made of wool, of cotton, and of leather, as may be desired. There are grains and nuts, as well as milk and honey; there are berries and melons. All of these, provided for the human body, tell of God's gracious care over the body which He made.

Who can doubt His love when we think of these provisions? For our enjoyment, He has provided flowers of every hue and color, and perfumes of such delightful fragrance as makes glad the heart of man. God has provided metals for man's use, some that are soft and decorative, beautiful and bright for adorning the person, others that are hard and heavy, such as iron and copper. He has given us very light-weight aluminum, besides gases of many kinds which serve useful purposes. God has withheld nothing from us.

Christ Reveals God's Kind Thoughts

Again Christ informs us in this verse that God has kind thoughts toward men. If we look at the condition of men and the state of society, we might well marvel that God could or does love at all. Why should He love men? Why should He not have hard thoughts toward men? The Soviet Republic has sought to exclude the things of God from Russia, and still God continues to send His sunshine and His rain upon that people, and to give them bread and flesh as well as every other blessing which He so graciously bestows upon everyone.

God is kind to men. His thoughts are thoughts of peace toward us. He would have us live without worrying. He would have us sing without sighing. He would have us serve without suffering. His Word describes quite fully His way of peace and gladness. He warns us against the things which break the heart and wreck our civilization. Those who believe Him and obey Him live happy lives and die happy deaths. It is those who disobey and refuse and reject the kind thoughts of God who suffer and sorrow and sink in the outer darkness. God's kind thoughts extend toward us individually and in the family relationships and in our national associations and in our international obligations. God has gracious thoughts of sweetest peace for every heart that lives. How blessed it would be if we would believe His love, accept His Son, and take refuge under the precious blood shed on Calvary !

Christ Reveals That God is Omniscient

Only the Son could reveal this. Only one who is omniscient could know everyone in the world personally, and love every such one individually. No one else could love everyone else, because no one else could know everyone else. Our knowledge of people is quite limited. The most of us know comparatively few. We may stand on the street corner in our own city and watch the multitude pass by only to meet an occasional acquaintance. But our God knows each person on the globe. He knows you, He knows where you live, He knows your age and your occupation, and He knows what you are doing each moment. He is the omniscient God. Christ has said so in John 3:16. There are divers who work in the bottom of the sea and sailors who live in submarines. He knows each of them. There are tribes who live in the trackless wastes and forests of the Amazon Valley, unseen by the eyes of white men, and He knows them. There are prisoners in the dungeons of our penitentiaries and there are aged ones in the homes for the poor; each of these is under His omniscient eye and is known by name to Him. Were it not so He could not love each and every person in the world. The teeming multitudes of earth are to Him just like so many individual persons whose entire lives are open and naked before Him. Knowing all this He loves with an everlasting love; He loves You.

Christ Reveals God's Determination

It is clear from the words of our Lord that God will go to the extreme in His love for men and women. Surely some other way would have been found for the saving of men than the giving of His Son, if it were possible. God is so wonderful in His knowledge so mighty in His power, SO great in His ability that surely there would have been some other way provided to save men beside taking

Christ from the eternal throne to hang on the cruel cross, if it were possible. God found no other way. The Son whom He so dearly loved must be severely punished for the guilt and sins of men. The throne must be vacated, the cross must be occupied, and God's heart must be terribly torn, if men are to be saved from the guilt and power of sin. The extreme price must be paid, because the need was so desperate and the punishment was so severe.

God made a world for the blessing of men's bodies and then He made a cross for the blessing of men's souls. It was God's will that Christ should die. It was God's plan and purpose that Christ should leave the glory of heaven for the agony of Calvary. God took the One who made the angels and made Him lower than the angels. God took the One who was sinless and made Him to be sin for us. God took the One who was higher than the highest and let Him die between two thieves in shame and disgrace. God took the One who was almighty and let Him suffer and die in weakness.

God went to the limit in finding a way of salvation for us. He gave His Son!

Christ Reveals That God is Omnipresent

God can see everything. If this were not so, He could not use the word "whosoever." He must be present when the soul puts its trust in Christ. He must be there when life is given to a dead soul. He must be near to hear the cry of the troubled heart, whether it be in the mountaineer's hut, or on the deck of a ship, or in the cabin of the airplane, or deep in the mines of the earth. He must be near when the little child seeks the Saviour, or the soldier in the trench cries out for mercy. Every day, in many parts of the world, hearts are seeking and finding the living God. In every corner of the earth the Holy Spirit is giving the gospel of grace to darkened hearts and troubled souls, and God is giving life to those who and Christ. "The eyes of the LORD run to and fro throughout the whole earth" (II Chron. 16:9).

God is where the ravens are, giving them their food. God is where every Christian is, guarding, preserving, keeping, comforting, blessing. Each individual, wherever he may be, may find God near, if in the name of Jesus he comes with a believing heart and puts his trust in Him. God is commanding His blessing upon the mountain tops and in the desert places, for He causes His rain to fall "where no man is." God is where the sparrow is, for not one shall fall to the ground "without your Father." None can hide from His presence and none should want to hide from Him. How much better it is to hide in Him! He is the giver of "every good gift and every perfect gift" (James 1:17).

In order that each one in every place may receive His personal care and individual attention, God must be and is OMNIPRESENT. We cannot understand how it is so and it is not necessary that we do understand; it is quite sufficient that we believe. Let each one "practice the presence of God," trusting implicitly in that One who is near and ready to save through Christ Jesus our Lord.

Christ Reveals That God is Omnipotent

Only an omnipotent God can promise to preserve forever any and every human being who trusts in Jesus Christ. Death would seek to prevent; decay is antagonistic; time is an enemy; and the present ways of living would apparently deny any such preservation. Here is the word of the living God, "SHOULD NOT PERiSH." It is God's fiat. It is God's promise. It is God's word. God affirms that it is so and it is so. He has the power to save the soul, to preserve the life, to keep the whole person unto His heavenly kingdom. He is mighty to save and strong to deliver.

His omnipotence is revealed in history and is declared by prophecy. Creation is an outstanding proof and salvation is incontrovertible evidence of His omnipotence. Only an omnipotent God can transform the cannibal and make him a devoted, worshiping Christian. Only an omnipotent God can change the cruel criminal and make him a godly, Christlike citizen of the community.

GOD is OMNIPOTENT! He has power over all flesh and power over you. He sets up kings and destroys countries. He preserved His people Israel, while He blotted off the earth their enemies. He caused the walls of Jericho to fall at the sound of the trumpet, and closed the mouths of the lions when Daniel visited the den.

His omnipotence in John 3:16 is not found, however, in connection with creation, nor in preservation, but rather in salvation. Of course, the one whom He saves is also preserved by Him. He is omnipotent in saving and He is omnipotent in keeping the one whom he saves. Do not hesitate to trust Him. Lean hard upon Him. Take Him at His word. He has power to save and power to keep You.

Christ Reveals That God Desires Our Fellowship

In these words, "have everlasting life," is revealed this deep, loving desire of God's great heart. Human beings with only human life can never have fellowship with the eternal God, unless this gift of life from heaven is given to them on earth. Communion is based on similarity of nature. Horses like to be with horses, and they understand each other; sparrows love to be with sparrows, and they know each other; sheep love to be with sheep, for their language and their desires are the same. Sinners love to be with sinners, for their likes and dislikes are similar. Christians love to be with Christ for they all love Christ. They have His nature. They understand Him and know His language. They are born "from above," therefore they are at home in heavenly places and enjoy the fellowship of the heavenly Trinity.

In order that it might be so, He found a way whereby He can give His own life and His own nature to fallen men who believe in Him. Perhaps you have seen many to whom you would never care to give your nature, for they are repugnant to you. It may be that you have even expressed your opinion, saying how glad you are that they are not related to you. In looking down upon men, God desired that we should be related to Him, and so has called on men everywhere, and you in particular, to accept Jesus Christ, His Son, that thereby *you* may have this eternal life which links the Christian with eternal bands to the eternal Trinity.

Yes, God does want our fellowship! He has gone to the extreme in making provision, whereby you may have this blessed and beautiful relationship in Him. Take Jesus Christ today, make Him the Lord of *your* life, make Him the Saviour of *your* soul, then you will have fellowship with God now and forevermore.

CHAPTER VIII

THAT WONDERFUL LOVE IN JOHN 3:16

LOVE stories always attract our attention and hold our interest. The love story recorded in this verse is quite unlike all other stories, for the love described therein transcends all others in its loveliness, its beauty and the results it brings to the trusting heart. We shall consider several aspects of this love and trust it will win our entire devotion to the Lord of love.

Love at Its Loftiest Source

This love is from One who knows how to love. He is the Author of love. Love first came from His heart. This love is heavenly in character and is like its Author, without a flaw or a failure. This love can be depended upon at all times, and in every place, and throughout life's journey. This love is fragrant and sweet, filling and thrilling the heart with ecstasies of rapture. This love drives the clouds away. This gracious attribute of God is sufficient to heal every broken heart and relieve every distressed soul. This love is an affectionate heart love, a devoted love, a gripping love. This love is from the greatest Lover in the world, whose love can neither be measured nor weighed, nor can it be limited by any boundaries of men or demons.

We read of the length and breadth and height and depth of this measureless love. Its length is so great that it goes to the ends of the earth to and the object of its search. Its breadth is so great that it will go from east to west and from north to south to and the wandering one wherever he may be, to allure him and draw him and attract him to this lovely Lover of his soul. Its height is so great that it will go into the halls of learning, the palaces of princes, the homes of the mighty, those who live in what is called the upper strata of society, and there this love will plead its cause, yearning over the lost souls who live lavishly and suffer miserably. Its depth is so great that it finds its way into the dens of vice and sink-holes of shame, that there it may call in sweetest tones to the wretched wreck of a human life, and say, "Come unto me." This wonderful love is for you. Do accept it! Do believe it!

Love in Its Widest Range

This application is disclosed in those beautiful words, "so loved the world." Wherever we go this story may be told. Whoever we meet may hear this message of grace. Very few things are universal in character and all such are gifts from God. The sun is universal, and shines upon the just and upon the unjust. The rain is universal, and falls upon the gardens of the rich and the hovels of the poor. The breezes are universal, and bring their cooling blessings to the prince and to the pauper. So this love of God covers the entire world like a blanket.

If we should go to the islands of the sea, Aniwa, Aneitym, Borneo, Madagascar, or Iceland, that love is there. Hearts are there who have believed that love and been filled with joy and peace through believing. If we should go to the Alps, or Himalayas, or the Andes, or the Rockies, there we shall find mountaineers and miners who have heard the call of this love, have believed the "Good News," and have become children of God through saving faith in Christ Jesus.

If we should go through the railroad shops, the steel mills, the automobile factories, there too, both in the offices and in the shops, we would find men and women who have enthroned the God of love as the Lord of their hearts. If we should visit the homes of the aged, the homes for crippled children, or institutions for the blind, there, too, we would find both old and young who have heard the story of this love of God and have fallen in love with the God who so loved that He gave His Son. So wide is the range of this love that there is no place on the earth, nor above it, nor within it, where a living man can go that this love may not be found, where this love may not be received, and where this love will not bring sweet peace to the human heart.

Love in Its Deepest Manifestation

This blessed unfolding is described by our Lord Jesus in those beautiful words, "He gave his only begotten Son." We often measure love by the gifts that are given by the lover. Of course, where there is a deep, true love, the character of the gift is the measure of the ability of the lover. The one who is very rich may give a beautiful home, nicely furnished and fully equipped, as the mark of his love to the object of his love. That friend who is poor may love just as deeply and just as ardently, but must be content with giving some handkerchiefs, or perhaps a book, or a pencil. The gift is the measure of the wealth of the giver.

Sometimes, however, the gift is a mark of the great or the little devotion of the giver. The millionaire might give a little gift because his love is little. "God so loved–that He gave His–Son." The character of that gift tells us in unmistakable language of the character of His love. The value of that gift tells us of the wealth of the Giver. The permanence of that gift assures us of the eternal love of that great Lover.

In order that this love of God might meet the deepest need of the worst of men, Christ went farther–He was made sin. What mysterious words these are! Who can fathom them? How deep did He go when this became true of Him? Beloved, no matter who you are, nor where you are, nor what you are, Christ came down low enough, far enough, deep enough, to put His eternal arms of love beneath you. How you should love Him for it! How you should trust Him! How you should believe in Him! Never was there a love like this which could love the unlovely and love to the limit. Never was there a Lover like this One who could love the lost with an eternal love so great that He gave such a priceless gift as His own peerless Son. Is He YOURS?

Love in Its Highest Purpose

This intent of God's heart is revealed to our hearts by the statement of our Lord in those words "not perish . . . but have . . . life." This love of God is an unselfish love. He loves in order that He may give. We love in order that we may get. Every poor man would like to find a sweetheart who is rich, that he may obtain her dowry. Every poor girl would like to find a rich sweetheart, that she might obtain that luxury and ease through his riches which her heart so much desires.

It is natural for the human heart to desire to get and to hold all that it can find. But the great purpose in God's love is that He may give to us now and keep on giving forever. His first gift is the gift of natural life. Then He gives graces and talents for that life. He gives food and clothing for the comforts of that life. He gives fragrance and color and flowers for the enjoyment of that life. He gives the sun for light and coal for heat and electricity for power for the purposes and uses of that life. These, however, are not the highest purposes of His giving.

God's great purpose and love for man is found in the gift of Jesus Christ for the soul, for the heart, and for the mind. He would have us filled with joy and with peace, and this can only be obtained through belonging to Christ Jesus, the Lord. He would have us at rest about the judgment, and this can only be brought about by saving faith in the Person and work of Christ at Calvary. His present work on the throne relieves us from our fears, and the Word of Christ in the Bible dispels our doubts. What indescribable love is this! What a majestic purpose was in the heart of God !

CHAPTER IX

SEVEN PRECIOUS TRUTHS IN JOHN 3:16

WE apply the word "Precious" to jewels and to babies. It describes that object which is dear to our hearts, either because of relationship, or because of its potential or actual value. Here in John 3:16 are seven "precious" truths. Surely we should treasure them as a priceless asset to our souls.

A Sacred Person

This blessed One is brought before us for the attention of our hearts and the meditation of our minds as we read the word "GOD." The Lord Jesus immediately takes our attention in this passage to the most wonderful and holy Person in all the universe. We are invited to think of Him, to look at Him, to meditate on Him, to lean on Him. to listen to Him. to consider Him. and to heed His words. What a blessed privilege it is for mortal man to know the eternal God!

God dwells in light unapproachable, as well as in darkness impenetrable. He dwells in the high and holy place, which no human eye has seen and no human hand has reached. He rides upon the wind and walks upon the clouds, where no human foot ever has or can tread, God is a holy God. No iniquity can dwell in His presence; no sin can touch His holy throne. His eyes are too pure to behold iniquity. He sits upon a white throne unspotted and untouched by the wickedness of men. Without formality, Christ Jesus introduces us to this serene and sacred Sovereign of the universe.

By the word of His mouth He placed a billion stars in their sockets of blue. By the breath of His mouth He made the myriads of fish in the sea. At His command there sprang into being the endless varieties of beetles and bugs, butterflies and birds, and at His command they are fed, kept, and reproduced. This great and majestic God, mighty in His power and matchless in His beauty, is revealed to us by these wonderful words of our precious Lord in John 3 :16.

"That Thou shouldst love a wretch like me,

And be the God Thou art,

Is darkness to my intellect,

But sunshine to my heart."

A Strong Passion

Love for lost men is the outstanding characteristic of God, and is revealed to us in the words "so loved." Love is said to be the strongest passion in the world. Love will overcome every obstacle and find the object of its love, though it traverse sea and land, mountain and valley, shop and home. The lad who was kidnapped had a father who loved him. Every force of the law, every instrument of the government, every human device that was obtainable, was commandeered for the purpose of finding the son whom the father loved. When a message was received demanding a tremendous ransom, the father immediately made arrangements to fulfill the demand, and did everything possible to obtain the money and deliver it to the abductors in the manner prescribed. Love paid the price to obtain the person that was loved.

Love will pursue its object in every possible way; by train and by auto the chase is made; by ship and by airplane the chase continues. Neither time, nor distance, nor the elements will interfere with this pursuit. Love schemes and plans in order to be with the object of its devotion. Love will risk health and wealth, possessions and positions, and will make any sacrifice, if it can only have that one on whom it has set its desires.

Here in John 3:16 is revealed the supreme love of all loves. It is the strongest of all loves, because it has accomplished the greatest ends. This love was willing to give the most marvelous of all gifts. This love reached to the highest throne to give a love gift to the worst of men, the lowest of sinners. This love loves all between the highest and the lowest; none are omitted, all are included. This love is for You

A Sinful People

These are the objects of this strong passion in the sacred heart of the eternal God. Sin has wrecked the lives of men. Sin has penetrated the palace of the king, the home of the peasant, and the houses of those in poverty. Tears attest its presence, sighs acclaim its cruelty, graves announce its ferocity. The presence of the police proves the presence of sin. Courts prosecute it; jailors seek to correct it; doctors treat it; the world's wealth pays for it.

Sin penetrates and permeates all society. Sin infects and afflicts. Sin fills the battlefields with the dead and asylums with the demented. Sin creates orphans and widows and fills graveyards. Sin wounds but never heals; sin brings sorrow without a solace. Sin cries constantly for more, it has an insatiable greed, it is never satisfied. Sin cares not for the damage it causes and recognizes no master nor law. Sin strikes at God's throne, and is an enemy of righteousness and of the rights of others. Sin has its devotees everywhere—alert, persistent, cunning, and zealous. Its advertisements are everywhere—attractive, alluring, colorful, and exciting.

Sin calls for the skill of the artist, the painter, the carpenter, the inventor, the musician, the printer, and the manufacturer. Sin lays a heavy toll on its participants to pay the bill, and then cruelly demands payment. The shores of time are strewn with the wreckage of sin, and the debris of many walls built by men to stop its progress and hinder its course is seen on every hand. Sin is the most prized of all possessions. Kings will lose a crown and forfeit a kingdom for it. Wise men will prostitute their wisdom to enjoy it. Wealthy men will fling away their riches to obtain it. Those who seek for it will die for it, will break up the finest home for it, will sever the dearest ties for it, will cast away their health and honor to obtain it. Men will forfeit all that is good and true and noble and pure, for a brief hour upon its bosom. Men will ignite an unquenchable fire, and face the dark portals of an endless hell, for a sip from the cup of sin. Oh, the awfulness of sin!

Great foundations have been established to study its causes and to effect a cure. The greatest minds are conscripted to invent ways and means of successfully combating it. The skill of the physician, the care of the nurse, and the services of the druggist are called upon to extinguish the flames of sin, and to repair the damage which it has wrought. Business men are against it; society is against it; teachers are against it; parents are against it; but among all of these we find no cure. God is against sin; Christ is against sin; the Holy Spirit is against sin; the Bible is against sin; the Church is against sin.

In the beautiful verse we are considering is disclosed God's remedy for a SINFUL PEOPLE. Only the love of God can conquer sin; only the blood of Christ can wash it away; only the Holy Spirit can prevent it; only the Word of God can supplant it.

God gave Christ to save you from its penalty, and now Christ will give you His life to save you from its power. The Holy Spirit gives you His Word to save you from its deceptions. Is sin driving you, or are you driving it? Are you saved from it, or condemned by it? Are you for it, or against it? Do you encourage it, or deny it? Do you feed it, or fight it? Do you hate it, or love it? God's remedy for sin is Calvary. God's reward for sin is the lake of fire. A sinful people may become a saved people, because of the strong passion of this sacred God.

A Striking Proof

The evidence of God's rich provision for a sinful people is given to us in the words of Christ: "He gave his only begotten Son." How often the question is asked, "How do I know that you love me?" Love must be shown; love must be proved; love must be experienced. God could have told us that He loved us and given no other evidence than the great gifts of creation. God could have said that He loved us and left us to believe it or to doubt it as we might choose.

God knew the frailty of the human mind and heart. God knew the desire of men to realize and to understand by His senses. Therefore, God has given us an unmistakable, undeniable, and unavoidable proof of the secret love that was in His heart, which He desired to reveal to us openly. Is it proof that you want? Then look at Bethlehem and the manger, or at Calvary and the Cross or at the crown on Christ's head in the glory. Do You want still further proof? Then go with Him into the wilderness as He spent forty days among the wild beasts and was tempted by Satan that He might prove to you that He can safely be trusted as the sinless Saviour of men

You may have still further proof of His love if You will go with Him to Gethsemane, and see Him in agony and anguish of spirit, lying prone upon the ground, suffering because He was about to take *YOUR* place Do you know of anything more that He could have done which would convince you of His great love for you? What further proof would you like to have? What additional evidence do you demand? What other facts do you ask, in order that your heart may be fully convinced that God loves you and has provided for you in Jesus Christ a perfect Lord, a sufficient Saviour, and a wonderful salvation?

A Simple Plan

The plan as portrayed in John 3: 16 is found in those two words, "whosoever believeth." God could have put the way of salvation upon a very expensive basis. Salvation is worth it. Is heaven not a valuable present? A priceless goal? is it not worth more than we are able to comprehend to escape the wrath to come and receive the love of God? is it not priceless beyond compare to receive forgiveness of sins here and now, and thus avoid the great white throne judgment?

When such a tremendous salvation, so valuable so precious, so wonderful, is to be obtained, it would have been quite in keeping if God had priced it at a very high valuation and demanded some great thing from men, in order that they might obtain it. It is because of God's love that He has made the plan simple. If salvation should only be offered to those who obtain certain scholastic degrees, then untold multitudes would never have an opportunity to be saved. Many in enlightened lands do not have the mental capacity to earn a degree, but God's salvation is for them. Millions live in the darkness of heathendom where colleges are not available, and where educational institutions of all kinds are unthought of, but God's salvation is for them. Many who have the mental ability do not have the financial resources whereby they may go to college and obtain a degree, but God offers His salvation to them. There are those who are afflicted with crippled bodies or with disease and who are, therefore, unable to attend any kind of an institution of learning, but they, too, are included in God's simple plan of salvation.

If salvation were obtained by lifting up the hand five times towards heaven, then those who are paralyzed would be shut out. If salvation should be offered to those who will walk in a straight line for fifteen feet, then all the cripples and the bedridden would be hopeless, for they could not fulfill the condition. If salvation should be on sale for a nickel or a dime, then millions could not have it, for multitudes have no money and never see any money. God has made the plan so simple that He may include all and exclude none, and that this great gift of eternal life may be within the reach of every living person, and may not be out of reach of a single soul.

How we should thank God for this simple plan! God grant that we may be simple enough ourselves to take with simplicity and by simple faith this simple plan which brings such blessed and eternal results. "He that hath the Son hath life" (I John 5:12).

A Sure Pledge

This pledge is given to every believer in Jesus Christ –to everyone who takes God at His word. This token of truth, this proof of fact is extended to us in these beautiful words, "should not perish." How do we know that the believer will not perish? Because we have His word for it. What greater pledge could we have than the word of One who cannot lie? What greater assurance could we have than the word of the eternal God who has never failed? His Word is immutable and imperishable. There is not a shadow of doubt or of darkness in His Word. "God is not a man, that he should lie, . . . hath he said, and shall he not do it? or hath he spoken, and shall he not make it good?"

The Word of God standeth sure! No one can alter it and nothing can change it. If He said "should not perish" to one who is a believer in Jesus Christ, then that believer will never perish. There is no doubt about it, nor is there any question. God will keep His word! God will perform His promise! God will maintain the truth of the words which He has spoken!

When Napoleon said to the brave soldier who saved his life, "Thank you, Captain," the private soldier became a captain immediately. The word of the Emperor was sufficient. The word of the supreme commander was also recognized by the other officers, and the private soldier was immediately received as one of the captains of the regiment.

When Wellington wrote "I will pay" beneath the list of the soldier's debts, as the soldier was sleeping, that burdened soldier knew that his commanding officer would lift the load from his heart and would pay his obligations. The general's word brought peace to the troubled private.

The burdened nobleman believed the word of Christ and went his way in peace, believing that his son was cured. He had only the word of his Lord, nothing else; nothing else was needed. This story is told in John 4:46-53. The word of our God is a sufficient pledge to every trusting heart. "The word of the Lord endureth for ever" (I Peter 1:25).

A Sterling Possession

The gift of life is the blessed present portion of every true believer in the Son of God. The possession of eternal life is the greatest possession possible to a human being. Other possessions may be taken from us by thieves and robbers, but no one can take Christ from the believing heart. Other possessions fade and fail, rust out, or wear out, but this blessed possession grows richer and rarer, brighter and more beautiful as the years go by.

Some possessions become a burden as taxes increase, but this blessed possession lifts the load from heavy laden hearts and makes the burden lighter. This possession is for eternity and prepares the Christian for that long experience in the heavenly kingdom. Other possessions cease their usefulness at the grave, but this possession is of value in the sunset days, when the shadows are falling, as well as in the early years of life. This possession enriches the soul, even when the riches of earth abound, and it also fills the heart with rest, the mind with peace, and the soul with joy, even when riches make themselves wings and flee away.

This priceless portion satisfies the craving of the heart when the feet fail to carry the body, and the eyes fail to see the light; when the ears can no longer hear, and the tongue cannot discern between sweet and sour; even then He still remains a precious portion for the heart of the trusting saint. To have Christ is to have life. Christ is our life. The life of God is in the Son of God. "He that hath the Son hath life." God gave Christ to you, so that in having Him you would have this sterling possession of eternal life. This possession links you with God. This possession equips you to enjoy God. This possession makes it possible for you to live with God. This possession will give you an understanding heart that can understand God. God grant that you may make Christ Jesus your own, so that with Him you may have everlasting life forever.

CHAPTER X

THE BLESSEDNESS OF THE GREAT GIFT

GIFTS allure and attract all through life. The old folks delight in gifts as do the children. Not only do we consider the one who gave the gift but its value as well, and delight to know that we have been remembered. Our Lord has gladdened our hearts by telling us of God's great love-gift, and we shall notice some interesting things about this gift.

The Author of the Gift is God

We always consider the source of love. We will not accept love from some people, it is abhorrent to us. We deliberately prevent others from loving us, because it would be improper to do so. Love from some sources would be a thing to be rejected and despised. Love must come from a person whose social standing is satisfactory to us, whose personality is pleasing to us, whose personal characteristics are suited to us, and whose offer of love is acceptable to us.

The Author of this great gift of love is none other than GOD Himself. This love should be appreciated by every man and heartily reciprocated, because His character is stainless, spotless, pure, and true. His holiness is unsullied. He is tender and kind beyond compare. He is more beautiful than the lilies which He has made. He is more graceful than the deer which He has created. He is stronger than the lion which He has formed. He is more wonderful than the glowing sunset or the mighty Alps. This is the One who has given us His love-gift, Christ Jesus.

This is the One whose love knows no boundary line, no race, color, social distinction, or nationality. He is the Author of this gift. His eternal grace and the indescribable beauty of His gift partake of these same wonderful characteristics. As He offers us His gift, no one can deny that the Author is Himself, wonderfully attractive and delightfully precious to the heart of everyone who knows Him.

The Incentive of the Gift

This gift was prompted by LOVE in the heart of God. Not all gifts are given for this purpose. Sometimes gifts are given because some favor is desired. At other times gifts are given to blind the mind of the judge. Sometimes nations will give great gifts to other nations, in order to make them an ally in the event of war. Gifts are given to pacify anger and to restore fellowship. Gifts are also given in order to pave the way for requests which are to follow.

The incentive of the gift in John 3:16 is just the pure love of God. with no ulterior motive whatsoever. How gracious God is and how wonderful is His love in that He loves those who are mere creatures of His hand, quite unable to enrich Him in any way, or to add to His glory, or His beauty, or His majesty! The only incentive is our need. He sees us wrecked and ruined by sin. He sees us coming far short of the glory of God. He sees us in our pollution, nakedness and wickedness, and it is while we are yet sinners of the deepest dye, both in our characters and in our actions, that He loves us. He gave Christ Jesus for us because of His great love.

In His holiness He certainly does not need us who are so sinful. In His deity He certainly does not need us who are so finite. You may search the world in vain for any other incentive of this gift, for you will find none, except the sovereign free love of God.

The Content of This Gift

The gift is none other than the PERSON of His own blessed Son. A mother with her new-born baby looks into its sweet little face and calls it Dorothy, God's gift. How happy that mother is to have for her very own a wee, tiny bit of humanity! This little one, however, may grow up to bring heartbreaks and heartaches to that mother. But God's great gift did not, does not, cannot break a human heart.

He came to mend broken hearts, and to bind up the bruises. There is no possibility of injury or harm in Jesus Christ. He brings only blessing to that one in whose heart He comes to dwell. The gift of money may lead to riotous living, but the gift of Christ leads to righteous living. One may tire of another's gifts, but this gift grows more precious and more wonderful as the possessor learns to know Christ better. Christ is not a dormant gift, but becomes quite active in the life of that one who possesses Him. Christ never becomes a burden as some gifts do, but lifts the burden from the heart that trusts Him. Christ is never a bother in the home where He comes to dwell. He is never in the way. He always brings with Him the sunshine of heaven, the blessing of God, the fragrance of eternity.

This gift never fails to fulfill every requirement of the soul and of the life. This gift is sufficient for every emergency and fits into every situation. This gift is unsearchable. The more you examine Him, or analyze Him, or test Him, the more wonderful He becomes, and the better is the beauty of His character brought to light. When you first accept Him, you only begin to know Him.

The Universality of the Gift

There are gifts which are valuable in themselves but which have no value to the recipient, because of conditions which may exist. A very fine palace and garden might be given to one who is blind and paralyzed, but he never could enjoy the blessedness of such a great gift. A beautiful piano might be given to one who is deaf, but he could not enjoy the music which would come from those strings. A very fine suit of clothes might be given to one who is entirely too small to fill the suit and he could not wear it. An expensive pair of glasses might be presented to one whose eyes they do not flt, and they would be useless. It is not so with this gift of God.

The gift of Jesus Christ is light for the blind. He is a Physician for the sick; He is a Comforter for the sorrowing; He is a Guide for the lost; He is a Saviour for the condemned: He is a Lover for those who are heartbroken; He is a Shepherd for His sheep; He is a Rock of Ages for the weary. He takes the little children in His arms, and confounds the doctors of the law with His wisdom. He can talk of fishing to the discouraged fisherman, or tell Nicodemus of the need of a great spiritual transaction. He is universal in His care, universal in His love, universal in His sufficiency. He is able to take care of you, if you will let Him be God's gift to You.

The Appropriation of the Gift

This truth calls upon us to believe in Christ Jesus. In this way we take Him, we accept Him, we receive Him—all of which means one and the same thing. You come to this blessed gift and find in Him the solution of your every problem. You at once appropriate Him for yourself. You turn your cares over to Him, commit yourself to Him, deliver yourself up to Him, and let Him be your Lord and Saviour.

A gift is of no value until it is appropriated. A friend might give you a beautiful automobile, but it would be of no value to you, nor would it render you any service, unless you believed the kindness of your friend and accepted the lovely gift. So with God's great gift of Jesus Christ. He must be appropriated. The rich can do no more, and the poor may do no less. The educated and the illiterate must meet together on the same level in this matter. Each one must appropriate the gift for himself. Each must adopt the gift personally. God says, "He that hath the Son hath life; and he that hath not the Son of God hath not life."

There were many who thronged Christ in Galilee and pressed upon Him in the crowd, but only one suffering woman accepted Him. She appropriated His healing power, and believed in His loving heart. God has given the gift; He wants you to take Him for yourself. God has given the Son; He waits for you to receive the Son. God has the blessing of salvation, forgiveness, and heavenly relationship all in the experience of appropriating

Jesus Christ. Be sure that *you* do it, my friend. Do not hesitate, do not equivocate; make that blessed gift your own while God is offering Him to you.

The Blessedness of the Gift

Here we find another wonderful blessing which we should consider carefully. Really, there are many beneflts; their number is countless, limitless. Through all eternity, in heaven as well as on earth, we shall be finding and enjoying the benefits of the gift of Jesus Christ.

There are unspeakable beneflts in belonging to God, for those who trust Christ become children of God, while those who do not accept Him are the children of wrath. There is the beneflt of having the life of God in the soul, for "he that hath the Son hath life." There is the benefit of having forgiveness, for in Him "we have redemption through his blood, even the forgiveness of sins, according to the riches of his grace." There is the beneflt of heavenly fellowship, for God has called us into the "fellowship of his Son Jesus Christ our Lord." There is the benefit of escaping the terrible judgment to come, for everyone who accepts this gift "cometh not into judgment, but hath passed out of death into life" (John 5: 24). There is the benefit of escaping the wrath of God, for "we shall be saved from wrath through him" (Rom. 5:9).

The benefit of living a life that shall never end, in the companionship and fellowship of Christ and all the saints, is a beneflt more valuable and precious than any other possible blessing of earth. In these few words, Christ gives us the greatest revelation the human heart could have: "NOT PERISH . . . BuT . . . HAVE . . . LIFE."

To have Christ is to become Christlike. To have Christ is to be taken from Satan's family and brought into God's family. To have Christ is to be linked with glory. To have Christ is to have an entrance into the presence of the Father. To have Christ is to cease the sighing and to sing the songs of heaven. How priceless are His beneflts! How precious beyond compare! No wonder the scripture says about those in Christ, "How shall he not with him also freely give us all things" (Rom. 8:32).

CHAPTER XI

JOHN 3:16 AND THERE IS NONE GREATER

WE should expect that there is little to be said after Christ has spoken. It is true that in John 3:16 the Lord Jesus has brought before us, by His conversation with Nicodemus, all that the heart could desire and all that the soul can need. We will find that this is true as we consider some of the great things in this passage.

The Greatest Motive

This actuating power is seen in the words, "GOD SO LOVED." Motives have always moved men. It was a motive that put the Panama Canal through a continent. It was motive that designed and built the tubes under the Hudson River. It was motive that enabled America to gain her independence. Nations have motives. Individuals have motives. You have some motives in your own life. In this verse, we find God's motive. The motive that led to the humiliation at Bethlehem, the motive behind the great transaction at Calvary, was the love of God–"For God so loved."

Usually, when a gift is given by a stranger, the question arises concerning the motive which prompted the gift. This unspeakable gift was given to sinners who had left God out of their counsels and ignored Him in their lives. Sinners are still doing it. Why should the wealthy God give such a wonderful gift to those who were strangers to Him? What was the motive behind it? The verse tells us it was love in His heart. It was a love that sinful men knew nothing about. They could never have known what was in God's heart, if the gift had not been given. The gift revealed the motive. It seems rather difficult to believe that a sinless and almighty God would love sinful men and women, who are so transient in their sojourn on earth, but it is true. He loves you and the motive behind the gift of Jesus Christ is nothing more or less than the wonderful love of His own peerless heart.

The Greatest Number of People

"WHOSOEVER" does not mean "EVERYBODY," but it does mean "ANYBODY." No other love in the world is like this. All other forms of love are quite exclusive in their character. Love usually embraces very few, and those few are very close to the heart. Human love is more exclusive than inclusive. It excludes nearly everybody and includes only a few. God's love is like Himself, greater, grander, all-embracing, and excludes none. He loves the greatest number, for when He said "THE WORLD" none were overlooked, none were omitted, none were left out. This fact alone marks the living God as being in an entirely different class than any human being.

The Greatest Gift

Presented to us in this beautiful verse, is the gift of a Person, and that Person, the Son of God, transcends all other gifts and eclipses all other giving. It is true that men do give great and expensive gifts, when their station in life and their resources permit it. Emperors have been known to give a petty kingdom to the one who married his daughter. Gems and jewels of great value have been given by men of wealth as wedding gifts to their brides. Solomon built a magnificent palace and gave it as a wedding present to Pharaoh's daughter, when she became his bride.

But all of these great gifts have disappeared. Families have been broken up and the valuable presents have fallen into the hands of others. God's gift of His Son is the greatest of all gifts, and the possessor never loses this gift. Even death cannot take from the heart and soul this priceless treasure.

The Greatest Blessing

That which we need above all else is "EVERLASTING LIFE." This blessing enables one to have joy in sorrow, and peace in the storm. This blessing keeps the soul at rest when all around seems to be sinking sand. This blessing brightens the way when the dark shadows of misfortune fall athwart the path. This blessing makes one more than a conqueror, because it is wrapped up in the Person of Jesus Christ. This blessing is Christ Jesus Himself, the Lord of glory. This blessing becomes dearer as the years roll by, and keeps the soul from sinking when the waves of adversity would seek to engulf it.

The Greatest Deliverance

Our hearts should rejoice in those words, "SHOULD NOT PERISH." Great fortunes perish, and so do the owners of them. Great estates perish, and so do the titled occupants. Great countries perish, and the inhabitants disappear. Great business establishments perish, and the next generation knows them no more. Great athletes perish, and their strong, healthy bodies go down in weakness and decay. Great generals perish, and others rise to wear their laurels. But the believer in Jesus Christ shall never perish. God will preserve him. Jesus Christ will save him. The Holy Spirit will support him. The angels of God will protect him. The Word of God will direct him. What a blessed deliverance it is to have the life preserved forever! To never perish is to always flourish. To never go down is to be always kept up. This is the rich portion; this is the wonderful deliverance of those who accept God's gift of His own Son.

The Greatest Sufficiency

It is quite enough that God should say, "WHOSOEVER BELIEVETH." Simple people need a simple formula. All of God's processes for the people are simple. He puts a few ingredients together and makes a potato; we never have to worry about it. He puts other ingredients together and makes the banana. This, too, is a simple process for Him. Other ingredients form the strawberry, while still others make table salt.

God sends the snow in the dead of winter, and in this simple and quiet way gives employment to thousands of men. He does it quietly and easily, while men sleep. God has so made the grain that it is not necessary for the farmer to plant the seed right side up in order that the plant may come up the natural way. No matter in what direction the seed may lie in the ground, the plant will always shoot up towards the sun. And so in the matter of salvation, we should expect that God would make it simple, and so He has. It is by simply believing, accepting, taking, trusting, and Christ Jesus is the object.

The Greatest Sincerity

God's integrity is revealed in this passage, because God has not spoken in a strange language, hard to be understood, but in most simple words. All the words are words of one syllable, except six of them, and these six are quite simple and easily understood. No scientific terms are used; there are no words which would require a dictionary to explain their peculiar meaning. None of the phrases found in this passage are ambiguous. Nothing in this verse could possibly be misunderstood. There is nothing unfinished in the words of our verse. Each statement is complete and is sufficient.

No one can have any question concerning the mind of God, nor the will of God, nor the purpose of God, after reading these beautifully simple words. Although Christ was conversing with a learned theologian, He did not use profound theological expressions which could only be understood by the university graduate. Christ spoke to this great and splendidly educated preacher in language so simple that children everywhere have been able to understand its message. Thank God for these few simple words which have transformed so many throughout the world. Let this simple message speak to your heart. God loved you; He gave His Son for you ; He wants you to accept His gift, and to have everlasting life.

CHAPTER XII

THIS WONDERFUL GIFT OF GOD

GIFTS are always free and yet they are sometimes accompanied by obligations which are not desirable. In John 3:16 there is presented to us a gift which carries wonderful opportunities and delightful duties with its marvelous privileges. The gift offered here is not an article but a wonderful Person. The Person whom we may receive as a gift is the wounded, risen, glorified Son of God.

A Personal Gift

The best gifts in the world are the gifts of persons. Have you never seen the love and joy that filled the eyes of that mother who for the first time held in her arms her very own sweet baby? What a thrill fills the soul! What a joy comes to the heart! What delight is expressed from the lips of that mother! Have you never seen at the wedding the radiant face of the bridegroom as he tenderly lifted the veil and kissed the sweetheart who has just become his own forever? The heart of a human being is only satisfied with a human being. No one wants to be a millionaire alone, he must be with others in whose fellowship he may enjoy the riches he has obtained.

God saw the need of the human heart, and provided a lovely Person to fit and meet the need of every soul. Christ Jesus is the gift for every nation. He satisfies the heart of the German and the Japanese. He brings perfect joy to the Italian or to the Ethiopian. Those in Sweden and those in the Sudan are equally satisfied with the gift of this Person. Each nation feels that Christ belongs to that nationality. Jesus exactly suits every sinner.

A Changeless Gift

This gift is one which does not change with the changing seasons. He is given and may be taken in the summer or in the winter, in the spring or in the autumn. It is not so with other gifts. We do not give overcoats in June, nor melons in December. The gifts of earth are suited to the seasons and to the circumstances. Different gifts are given according to the need which is manifested at the time. Not so with Christ! There is always the need for Him, in summer or in winter, in the sunshine or in the shadow, by day or by night. Christ is given and Christ may be taken at any time. There is never any season of the year or hour of the day when He is not needed, nor when He is withheld.

This lovely gift does not change with the times. If you will observe old photographs, you are amused at the strange hats that were worn in former days, the peculiar sleeves and the unusual cut of the coat. We say that those styles are out of date, and are not now in fashion. Christ Jesus is never out of date. He is always in fashion. The Christian graces which He bestows, and the salvation which He gives, are just as attractive and desirable today as in the years past. He adorns those who trust Him. He beautifies those who receive Him. He dignifies and makes honorable those who make Him Lord of the life. No form of education, nor of man-made religion has ever been found which will do for the soul and for the life what Christ Jesus will do. You should receive this gift. You should make Him yours while you may. He will make you a prince fit for the palace of heaven.

The gift of Jesus Christ does not change with the age of the recipient. The little lad who receives Him finds that He is adapted to all the needs of a little boy. The child's faith is honored by the mighty Saviour. Christ brings Himself into the scope and comprehension of the young mind of the lad, and as the years go by and maturity is reached, with all of its wisdom, knowledge, and understanding, still the Lord Jesus is just as dear, just as valuable, just as wonderful to the mind that is trained.

The beauties of Christ increase as the vision of the mind increases. The wonders of Christ increase as the conceptions and receptions of the mind increase. There are shallows in the revelation of Christ in which the little ones can wade, and there are depths in the person of Christ which the sages of earth have never fathomed. The length and breadth, the depth and height of the glorious beauties of Christ invite from the wisest of earth their closest scrutiny and their most profound study. Christ is such a gift that no one in all the world can comprehend Him to the full. Is He your gift? Have you trusted Him?

An Incorruptible Gift

Most of the gifts of earth deteriorate with time and with use. The gold ring, placed so tenderly on the maiden's finger at the marriage altar, wears out with the using, and becomes thin and worn with the years. The wedding dress must be soon laid away, for its materials are so thin and frail that a little use soon destroys its usefulness. The automobile, made of steel and wood, becomes damaged by the hazards of the road, wears out with the long mileage, and must be replaced. Houses become uninhabitable by reason of the storm, the wind. and the weather. Cities become buried in the sand because of the destroying winds from the desert. Ships strike hidden reefs and rocks, and flounder in the depths of the sea. Strong bodies fade and fall. Fine woods are eaten by the worms, and the best of books become powder by reason of air and dampness. Only Christ remains ! The Scripture has said, "They shall fail, but thou remainest."

A Precious Gift

Here is a gift for your heart and soul which grows sweeter as the years go by, and brighter with the passing seasons. Here is a gift that becomes more and more valuable, as you know Him better and need Him more. Here is a gift from whom you may receive daily comfort, constant care, and the ministry of mercy, when the heart fails from grief and disappointment.

With the gift of Christ Jesus there are no obligations, but there are privileges and opportunities. Once a quitclaim deed was laid on my desk. Upon examining it I found that a friend had deeded to me a splendid piece of property upon which there was a new apartment building large enough to accommodate six families. It was really a wonderful gift. I was quite surprised in receiving the gift from someone who was almost a stranger and at once inquired about the obligation. I soon discovered that there was a mortgage of $25,000.00 against the property, which would be due in a few weeks and which I must pay, if I kept the gift. Of course, I refused to accept the gift. The obligation was too great for me to meet.

Such is not the case with Christ Jesus. With this wonderful gift there is given the power and the privilege, the assets and the opportunities with which to meet every obligation. This gift will enrich you both as to your character and your conduct. It will enable you, both as to your service and your ministry. This gift leaves nothing to be needed, nor to be desired, for living "the life that wins." if you have never received this gift of His "Only Begotten Son," then do so now. He will not be a disappointment.

A Valuable Gift

There are gifts which prove to be of no value to those who receive them. I received a gift of a box of fruit from California, but the fruit had spoiled in transit and could not be eaten. Sometimes a gift of beautiful china is received with some of the pieces broken. Furniture is given often times, but becomes damaged by scratching and breakage while en route. But there is no danger in receiving the Lord Jesus, for He is the perfect, wonderful, and blameless Redeemer, and can never be damaged.

You cannot have half a Christ, but you may have a wounded Christ. You cannot have a deflcient Christ, nor one who has been weakened or hurt or damaged by the centuries and countless enemies, for He is the perfect Saviour. If you receive Him, He will come to you in all His loveliness, and all the beauty of His character, and all the sufficiency of His work. This blessed gift will grow in value and appreciation, as He lives with you through the storms and sorrows of your life. No one who has received Him has ever been disappointed by Him. No one has ever taken Him and then found that He had no remedy for their distresses. This gift brings forgiveness of sins, salvation for the soul, and life everlasting.

An Abiding Gift

With all the gifts that you have received, it has been necessary to hold on to them, but here is a Gift who will hold on to you. You find it wise to surround your precious gifts with guards, with locks, with vaulted walls, with officers of the law, and with bells to give the alarm of danger. You must exercise great watchful care over the things you hold dear. Your jewels, your gold, your watches, and your money are hidden away in a safe place, carefully protected from thieves and robbers. But the Saviour is a gift that guards and protects the one who owns Him. He will keep you safely in the hollow of His hand. He will preserve you from sin and Satan. He will be a hiding-place from the strife of tongues and a shelter from the raging storm. He will keep you as a mother guards her babe, and as the lion protects her cubs. You will become His peculiar treasure, whom He will preserve with His own mighty hand. Therefore you should take refuge in Him at once, if you have never done so. Trust Him now and trust Him fully.

CHAPTER XIII

THESE ALL BELONG TO GOD

IN John Three Sixteen, our Lod Jesus has presented to us seven things that belong entirely to God. None of them is a product of earth, none is the result of man's inventive genius, none is the consequences of man's moral program. The Love that is mentioned is God's Love. It is as pure as He is pure. It is as wonderful as He is marvelous. It is as glorious as His own unapproachable presence. It is as eternal as His everlasting throne. It is not like our love which is restricted in it expression, but rather His love goes out to ever human being in every state of sinfulness.

This World is God's World

He conceived it, He designed it, He created it, He formed it, He started it on its path in His great universe. He planted it in its orbit. He created 'its ninety-two chemicals'. He formed the crooked serpent, the peculiar giraffe, the horrible crocodile, the graceful deer, and then He made man upright after His own image.

This is a world in which there are fragrant flowers to please, beautiful colors to adorn, wonderful metals to enrich, delightful food to satisfy, and every good and perfect gift which the human heart could possibly desire. It is indeed God's world and He had a right to place man here. He had a right to devise a way of salvation for man when he sinned in the beautiful world, and He now has the right to demand that the human heart bow to His decisions.

God still delights in His creation, for it is His handiwork, and He still loves man, although he is a fallen being–ruined by sin. God hates sin, because He is holy; but He loves the sinner, because He is merciful.

This Gift is God's Gift

It is a great gift, because God is the giver. It is boundless, measureless, fathomless, timeless, and inexhaustible. This gift enriches the recipient. This gift is from God and has God's approval. Many times over do we read that the Father sent the Son.

The giving of this gift originated in God's heart. No great inventor thought up this wonderful plan. This gift was not the product of some program of man. No human scheme, no human project developed this great and lovely gift. It was provided by God.

The giving of this gift proved that God was lavish in His loving and liberal in His giving. He was gracious in inviting all to accept this gift. He is powerful in preserving those who receive this gift. He is lordly in saving those who possess this gift.

This Son is God's Son

No other Son would do. David had a great son, Solomon, but he could not be God's Saviour. Solomon had a son, Rehoboam, but he could not be God's gift to men. Emperors have had sons and so have statesmen; great artists have had sons and so have musicians; great generals have had sons and so have educators; but none of these sons could save men's souls. Obscure fathers have had illustrious sons, and famous fathers have had noted sons; but none of these could save your guilty soul and mine. The only Son who can save guilty sinners from their sins is God's Son. Those who have the Son have life: all others are dead in their sins, because they have not life.

This Faith is God's Faith

The faith in any human heart which lays hold of God's Son is the faith produced in that heart by the Holy Spirit through the Word of God. Saving faith in the Son of God is not the product of the universities of earth. No college course can produce saving faith. No educational garden can grow this plant of faith. No mines of earth ever held the secret of faith. "Faith cometh by hearing, and hearing by the word of God." Its author and finisher is God. It comes down from God into the human heart and lifts that heart up to God. God's faith leads the repentant soul to believe God's Word and never to doubt Him. God's faith leads the believer to receive Christ and never to reject Him. God's faith leads the Christian to love Christ and never to leave Him. Those who have God's faith are the "whosoever wills." Those who do not have this faith are the "whosoever will-nots." God's faith causes men to be faithful followers of the Lamb.

This Preservation Which Keeps the Believer from Perishing is God's Preservation

Unless God preserves the Christian, he will never be kept from perishing. The best of men and women, surrounded with the best of human preventive measures, have gone down in utter defeat. No human remedy has ever been found for the wickedness of the human heart. Men in every generation have sought to preserve the human soul and the human body, but all such efforts have failed. It is true that smallpox, yellow fever, and typhoid fever have been almost eliminated from our communities, but other hazards have developed in their place, and the average human life is still some sixteen years below the allotted threescore years and ten.

This Life That is Given is God's Life

It does not have a human origin. It cannot be produced by human means or efforts. No amount of culture or reflnement can give eternal life. No amount of training or thinking can implant eternal life in the soul. Only God can impart it. Only the Holy Spirit can implant it. Only Jesus Christ can make it possible.

There are many phases of human life, but there is only one life from God. This eternal life given to the recipient is God's nature. It makes one hunger for God. It enables one to understand God. It causes one to think God's thoughts after Him. This life is eternal, as God is eternal.

Since this life is God's life, it can only be given by God. No church can control it. No human being can impart it. No system of religion can produce it. No ecclesiastical fiat can confer it. God alone has complete control of it. This life is in Christ Jesus, and those who have Him have life: those who do not have Him do not have eternal life, but remain dead in their sins.

CHAPTER XIV

CHRIST IS BETTER THAN OUR BEST

IT SEEMS to be the nature of men to depend upon their own merit for favor with God. All human systems of religion are based upon human merit in some form. Men's thoughts, men's deeds, men's actions, men's gifts are all made to bear favorably upon man's acceptance with the righteous Judge. Christ strikes a blow at this false faith in John 3:16, as we shall see in the present chapter.

This Love of God is Unmerited in Its Object

The world is the object of the love of God in John 3: 16, although it is the world that hates God. The world ignores God, it defies God, it is entirely contrary to God. The political world does not want Jesus Christ in any of its plans and schemes. The educational world does not want God's gift, nor does it make any provision in its program for the Person, or the Work, or the Word of the great Trinity. The financial world has no time to consult with the Lord Jesus, nor with the Holy Spirit, nor with the Scriptures concerning its transactions among men.

Sinners wish to run their own way. Religious sinners are content with man-made religions. All men everywhere have forfeited all rights to come under the beneficent influence of the love of God.

All men are under condemnation and the natural mind is enmity against God through wicked works, so that this love of God is entirely unmerited and undeserved.

This Love of God is Unsought in Its Action

Men do not seek God's love, but they do seek His gold and silver, His health and wealth, His peace and prosperity. They want His gifts, but they do not want Him. The soldiers gambled for the garments of Christ, while they crucified the Owner of the garments. They wanted that which belonged to Him, but they did not want HIM. "There is none that seeketh after God," but there are many who seek the things that belong to God.

God had to work sovereignly in bringing His love to men and in the giving of His Son. None were desiring it. None were seeking it, perhaps you are not seeking it even now. This blessing of God is unsought in the realms of human life. Men will spend much time and effort in seeking to obtain God's gifts. Some will go to great expense, others will risk their lives, and there are some who will spend their health in seeking for the prized possessions of God, the things which He has made, but His love is unsought.

This Love of God is Universal in Its Offer

There are no limits and no restrictions whatever in the offer which love makes and the gift which love gives. This love-gift of God, Christ Jesus, is available to everyone who lives and breathes. None are overlooked, none are despised, none are excluded, none are refused, none are forgotten. That blessed word, "WHOSOEVER," explains in fullest measure how universal is the offer of this love of God. It is universal in order that none may complain. It is universal in order that none may accuse God of being partial. It is universal that every mouth may be stopped at the judgment throne. It is universal that God's character may be maintained in unsullied holiness. It is universal that all may have an equal opportunity and privilege. Be sure, my friend, that you are included in this blessed universal offer.

This Love of God is Unbounded in Its Gift

The gift is Christ Jesus. He is the only Son of God, and yet He was given. He was the only heir of God, and yet He was sent. He was the only One in whom God could fully express and reveal Himself, and so He was not spared. "God spared not his Son." This Son was the dearest to the Father's heart. This Son was the mightiest in the Father's realm. This Son was the Creator of everything that was made. In all heaven and earth there was none so great as He, excepting the Father and the Holy Spirit, and they were not greater. This is the One who was given as a gift to sorrowing, suffering sinners. Surely this gift is unbounded. We cannot for a moment comprehend how great He is, how wonderful, how majestic, and how almighty. This love of God was indeed unbounded in giving such an unspeakable gift,

This Love of God Was Unfathomable in Its Depth

The Son had to come from the highest glory to the deepest humiliation. From the highest throne He came to the lonely stable and manger. The One who was Almighty on the throne in glory, became weak and weary as a man. This One who rode upon the clouds in His majesty and might was obliged to ride upon an ass in His weakness and meekness. The One who sat at His Father's right hand in highest glory must sit beside a sinful woman on the well-curb, tired, dusty, and thirsty. This One who could feed the thousands, after giving thanks for the five loaves and two fishes, left Bethany one morning and was hungry. This One who could say, "If any man thirst, let him come unto me and drink," cried out in the agony of Calvary, "I thirst." How unfathomable is the depth of this love of God!

This Love of God is Immeasurable in Its Ministry

"Should not perish" means a life of great profit and usefulness. Instead of the life fading and failing in unbelief, this love of God and this gift of Jesus Christ cause the life to shine more and more unto the perfect day. Because of this love, civilization has followed the Bible and the comforts of life have followed the gospel throughout almost the entire world. Where the gospel is reached, there is harmonious music; where the gospel is preached, there is soap and there are schools; where the Bible has gone, human kindness has been produced; homes for the aged have been erected; hospitals have been established; educational systems have been introduced.

No one can measure the extent nor the influence of the ministry of this love of God. Because of this we have transportation systems, and refrigerators, and typewriters. Because of this love, we may live together in large communities as contented friends. Because of this love, there are many public servants, such as doctors, nurses, druggists, policemen and school teachers. Because of this love we have bandages, anesthetics, protected foods, inspected milk, impounded water, and sanitary systems. No one can measure the length and breadth and depth and height of the influence of the love of God and the gift of Christ on this earth.

This Love of God is Unending in Its Character

Every other gift ceases to function. All the gifts of men must be laid aside at the grave. None can take with him the precious treasures, the heirlooms, the mementoes, or the souvenirs of the friendships of life. These all must perish, all must be left behind when the soul is called to go into eternity. All human love is born but to die. Death ruthlessly stops it, quarrels hinder it, misunderstandings disrupt it, distance cools it, time eradicates it. None of these is true of the great love-gift of John 3:16.

Everlasting life knows no ending. Eternal life never ceases. The life of God knows no cessation. This love is an unending as its Author. While He lives, we shall live. While He loves, we shall be loved. While He supports and protects, we shall be safe. None of the vicissitudes of life can hinder or harm this love. None of the dark clouds of adversity can hide us from this love. None of Satan's plans or programs can prevent this love from hovering over us and hiding us beneath its wings. This love of God, this Son of God, this gift of God is indeed unending in its character.

CHAPTER XV

GOD'S ATTITUDE REVEALED

GOD has been maligned and misrepresented throughout the centuries. Each false religion presents God in a light that is contrary to the revelation of His Word. In the passage we are considering, the Lord Jesus clears up all doubts as to the character and attitude of God and we should praise Him for thus illuminating our minds about the Father.

God's Attitude Toward the World

It is an attitude of love. God did not need to take this attitude. He could have been a severe Judge, punishing quickly and relentlessly those who broke His laws. God could have imposed severe penalties, and punished with cruel blows those who disregarded His Word and disobeyed His laws. God could have killed off the weakest and blessed the strongest. God could have established a very drastic set of laws with certain penalties, and forced men to walk uprightly through fear of being punished. But none of these things are true of our God. His attitude has been and still is one of lovingkindness and tender mercy. "GOD So LOVED." it does not say "GOD So HATED." How our hearts should bow in adoration to that One whose whole attitude toward us is one of love, and whose planning for us declares so plainly that His thoughts are of the deepest and sweetest love toward His creatures!

God's Attitude Toward Sin

He gave Christ to save us from its power. He gave Christ to save us from its presence. God is against sin. God's Word is against sin. God's Son is against sin. God would save us from the terrible consequences of sin. God loves the sinner, every kind of sinner, and He would save that sinner from the terrible consequences of his sinning.

God will not comfort the sinner in his sins, but He will save the sinner from his sins. God will not now condemn the sinner for his sinfulness, but will seek to convert the sinner unto holiness. God will not compromise with sin, for He has condemned it at Calvary in the body of His Son. God has revealed the awful sinfulness of sin by sending a sovereign Saviour in order to conquer this terrible enemy.

The horrible results of sin are indicated by the marvelous provision which God made to save men from it. God's perfect righteousness is revealed in this passage, because God was willing to make such a great sacriflce in order that the vilest sinner might have an abundant entrance into the holy of bones. God is against sin, are you?

God's Attitude Toward His Son

Although He loved His Son, He was willing to deliver Him up to death. Although He had enthroned His Son, He was willing to let Him go to Calvary's cross. Although He had made all things by Jesus Christ, He was willing for Christ to be crushed by the very things He made. Although the Lord Jesus was higher than the highest, God permitted Him, and in fact sent Him, to be made lower than the lowest. Although the Lord Jesus was the center of the worship and adoration of angels, God sent Him to be the center of the mocking and the scoffing, the spitting and the scourging of wicked men. Although Jesus Christ dwelt in the light unapproachable, the Father sent Him to be enshrouded in the blackest darkness. Although Christ had been the invincible Monarch of the great creation, God sent Him to hang helpless on the cruel tree. But God did not leave Him there; God has highly exalted Him, and has made Him both Lord and Christ. God has given Him a glorious name at which every knee shall bow and every tongue confess. Surely this attitude toward His Son should win your heart, for God gave up His Son to win You. Will it all be in vain as far as you are concerned?

God's Attitude Toward Believers

God has ordained that believers shall live with Him and for Him. God has provided for them, so that they may walk with God now and live with Him hereafter. God has given to them the very life that is in Himself, so that they may enjoy the things of God, delight, in His service, and feel at home in His presence.

God has planned in a miraculous way for believing men to be related to Him. He makes them His children. He makes them His heirs. He links them with unbreakable bonds, and binds them with eternal bands to Jesus Christ. He has ordained that wherever Christ is, they shall be. He has equipped them for His service here and hereafter. Believers can see the things which are unseeable and know the things which are unknowable. Believers have a life which feeds on invisible bread and drinks that living water, never tasted by human lips. Believers have the privilege of living in heaven now, for they are made to "sit together in heavenly places in Christ Jesus." Believers dwell in the secret place of the Most High, and abide under the shadow of the Almighty. This is heaven! it is a heaven on earth. It is a little foretaste of the real heaven which awaits us beyond the tomb. It is a sample of that which we shall enjoy when caught up to meet the Lord in the air. God has provided nothing but good for His children. He has given Christ in all of His fulness to His saints. "No good thing will He withhold from them who walk uprightly." in Christ we have the fulness of the Godhead bodily. In Christ we have the sufficient answer to every requirement of the human soul. Christ is our life. Christ is our peace. Christ is our salvation. If we have Christ, we are sufficiently supplied. How blessed it is that God has given to us in Christ Jesus all that is needed for this life and for the next. This is His attitude toward the believer.

God's Attitude Toward the Unbeliever

God rejects the man who rejects His Word. The unbeliever lives day by day by the forbearance and kindness of God. The life of the unbeliever is being lost. That which he says and does is not worth preserving. God's plan for the unbeliever is that he shall go out into the outer darkness. He shall be shut out from all of God's grace and goodness. He shall forever dwell with the lost. He shall forever hear only moans and groans. He shall throughout eternity endure the sighs and the cries of others who are unbelievers.

What a terrible word is that word "PERISH!" It was spoken by the loveliest of men, Christ Jesus, and He wasted no words. Christ did not play with human feelings. Christ did not make a mockery of the solemn things of eternity. Christ used this word with one of the world's best men, Nicodemus. He warned Nicodemus lest he should perish. He warns you, lest you should perish. He is not "willing that any should perish, but that all should come to repentance."

None of God's blessings are for the unbeliever. There is no mansion in glory for the man who doubts or denies the love of God and the Son of God. He must perish! God has said that he will perish. The law demands that he shall perish. This is God's attitude toward the unbeliever.

Beloved friend, if you are still an unbeliever, turn now to God, believe His Word, and accept His Son. " Step over the line and trust."

CHAPTER XVI

STRIKING ILLUSTRATIONS

THE products of the great manufacturing druggists are tested and tried before they are offered to the public. The results obtained by these tests guide the advertising department in their statements to the trade. John 3:16 has been tried in every kind of situation, has been applied to every kind of heart, and some of the results are given in this chapter. You, too, will find that God's remedy, thus appropriated by you, will be efficacious and sufficient.

Saved on a Plow Handle

A farmer boy in southern Missouri had attended a gospel service in the neighborhood and became interested in the welfare of his soul. The evangelist had been preaching on John 3:16 and was stressing the word "whosoever." This young man had lived a wicked life, and as his sins loomed up before him, he felt that his case was too bad to permit of his coming to Christ. He had always felt that only good people could be saved. He had never claimed to be very good himself, but he was quite sure that good people would be accepted of God. The more he compared himself with others, the more he felt the guilt of his sins and the hopelessness of his case.

One day as he was walking in the field behind the plow, his soul was in such distress that he stopped the horses, while he sat down on the plow to figure out a way of escape. He remembered that the preacher had stressed the word "whosoever." It did not say "whosoever is good enough," nor did it say "whosoever is nice enough," nor did it say "whosoever has just a few sins."

The more he thought of the word, the more clearly he saw the breadth of it. and saw the love of God in omitting any qualifying phrase. He said to himself, "If whosoever means anybody, then God certainly must mean me. If God gave Christ for sinners, He certainly must have given Him for me." He lifted his heart to God in thanksgiving and believed that the "WHOSOEVER" call included him. He accepted the invitation and trusted the Lord Jesus.

God gave the word "whosoever" to set at rest every question in any heart concerning his or her welcome into God's presence.

A Christian Worker But Not Saved

A solemn story was told me by a man who for years was quite prominent in Christian work throughout the United States. This friend said to me one day, "I have conducted Christian services for many years, and have been in meetings where the power of God was manifested and many turned to Christ. But throughout all of those campaigns, I have felt in my heart that I was not saved myself. This has been such a burden on my heart that I have come to you for help.

"Briefly, the story of my life is this: At about twenty or twenty-one, I was invited to travel with an evangelist to look after his various tabernacles. I accepted the position and thought that perhaps my presence in the meetings and the constant ministry of this friend would reveal the Saviour to me. But I did not find the Saviour, and was too proud to admit that I was not saved myself. Therefore, I have continued through the years pretending to be a saved man, when really I was not. Can you help me?" I directed his attention to John 3:16. "It is eternal life that you need, isn't it, my friend?" I said, as we finished reading the verse. He replied that undoubtedly that was his great need, and he would like so much to receive this life.

"You know this verse so well," I said, "that it is hardly necessary for me to explain it to you, but I will ask you to apply it to your own heart. Will you not, in your own room, on bended knees, tell the Lord Jesus of the hypocrisy and sham of your profession? Tell Him that you will accept Him now as the Lord of your life and the Saviour of your soul. Tell the Father that you accept His gift of eternal life, and that you trust yourself to His blessed Son. He will give you life at once, you will be born again, and will receive the desire of your heart."

My good friend went away to be alone with his Lord, that he might do as I suggested. He did kneel before the God whom he had served in ignorance. He did accept the living Saviour, about whom he had sung and preached throughout the land. Writing me later. he said, "I am now enjoying that sweet peace which I have long coveted, but have never known till now."

The Deacon Believed John 3 :16

A paperhanger came to my home recently seeking for peace. He had driven over two hundred miles to spend a little time with me, because two years before I had given a message in his city which convinced him that he was not saved at all. He was a deacon in one of the churches of his city, had held several church offices, and was well regarded as a fine Christian man in his community.

He told me his story and it is the story of many a misguided and darkened heart in religious communities everywhere. As a boy, his Sunday school class attended a revival meeting in his church, and through the urging of the Sunday school teacher he and others in his class went forward and united with the church.

He said, "I did this with others, but there was no change in my heart. Nothing happened to me. I seemed to be just the same boy afterwards as before, except that I became more religious than formerly, and took part in various exercises in the church. I have continued in this path until now, when I am fifty-one years old, but there is still no peace in my heart. "I often wondered whether anybody could really know if he were saved, and I comforted my heart with the thought that I had as much religion as others had, and was living a better life than many other professing Christians whom I knew." He had brought his New Testament with him, and so we opened to John 3:16. I asked him, "Would you like to be saved right now, and to know definitely that you are saved?" "Certainly," he said, "that is just what I came to see you about. If salvation is obtainable, I want it." We read the verse together, and then took it phrase by phrase. Our conversation ran along about like this:

"Do you think that eternal life is a present possession, or something that you obtain at the end of life?" "I suppose it comes at the end, if we deserve it."

"Will you read this verse again, and tell me what it says about deserving life, and obtaining it at the end?"

He read the verse and said, "It seems to come through believing, and it seems to be given right now.

I do believe, but I certainly do not have eternal life. What is the matter?"

"Would you like to tell me what it is that you believe."

"I believe every word of the Bible. I believe that Jesus is God's Son and that He is the Saviour."

"This does not satisfy your heart, does it?"

"No, and it never has."

I called his attention to the difference between believing the fact, and applying it to his own heart, and said to him, "If Christ is the Saviour of men, then you may safely trust your case to Him. He accepts all who come to Him, and applies the saving work of Calvary to those who believe that He did it for them. I wish you would tell the Lord Jesus that you do trust Him and that you rest on His finished work of the cross."

We knelt together at the sofa in the parlor of my home, and he said, "Lord Jesus, I do accept You for myself. I have always believed about You, but thought that Your work was for others. I now see that it was my own sins that You were bearing, and I believe that You blotted them out for me. I thank You for saving me this morning. I believe I am Your child, and that You have forgiven me."

As he said this, a new joy and peace came into his heart, and he left me with the assurance that he had passed from death unto life.

He Finally Believed "Whosoever" Meant Him

Another friend was saved through some very simple illustrations about John 3:16. He, too, was stumbling over the word "whosoever," and questioned whether it really included him. Our conversation was along these lines:

"If you saw a sign in a yard which said, 'Whosoever trespasses here will be punished,' would you believe that it meant you?"

"Certainly I would," he replied.

"If you saw a sign in an orchard which read 'Whosoever desires to do so, may eat of these oranges, but none may be carried away,' would you believe that it meant you?"

"Certainly I would, and I would help myself quickly."

"If you saw a sign on a bus which said, 'A free ride to the fair grounds for whosoever wants to go,' would you board the bus?"

"I would if I wanted to go to the fair."

"Very well," I continued, "God has said, 'Whosoever believeth in him should not perish.' Why do you not immediately trust in Christ Jesus, give yourself over to Him as you would to the bus driver, trust your case to Him as you would give your body to a doctor, and let this wonderful Son of God be your Lord and Saviour today? The word 'whosoever' was used by Christ, so that you would know that you were invited and included." I had turned to a passage with which he was familiar. As soon as we had begun to speak, another boy of about the same age came and sat on the other side of me to listen. for he, too, wanted to find the Saviour. After we had read the verse together slowly and with emphasis on certain words, I said to the first boy:

"Do you know to whom God gave His Son?"

"He gave Him to you," he answered.

The second boy replied, "I think He gave Him to us kids."

"That is right," I said. "It was to you that the Lord Jesus was given, but you have probably not made Him your own."

I noticed that the first boy had a ring on his finger and I asked whether it was given to him as a gift. He replied that he had worked for the money with which he purchased it. Then I asked if his trousers were given to him, and he replied that he had worked and earned the money to buy them also. The little lad did not have anything with him that had been received as a gift. Finally, I said to him, "Does the giving of a gift make the gift yours?" While he was thinking of my question, the lad to my right answered quickly, "You must take it, if it becomes yours."

"Quite so," I answered, "and Christ Jesus must be taken as a Gift, if He becomes yours. God has given Him to you, but He wants you to accept Him. You see, boys, I am a doctor, but I am not your doctor, am I?"

They both replied, "No."

"Why not?" I asked.

"Because we never took you," they replied.

This very answer seemed to illuminate their hearts and at once both the lads bowed their heads and told the Lord Jesus that they would take Him right then and there.

A Great Missionary Verse

Recently, I heard a missionary from Bolivia give a message on this passage as a missionary call. If GOD so loved the world, so should we. No part should be omitted. No people should be overlooked. No tribe or nation should be excluded from our missionary program. If God gave His Son to this sinning world, we, too, should give Him to the world. It is "light" that the heathen need, therefore God gave Christ, and we should give them Christ, who is the Light of the world. Men and women everywhere are perishing, perishing without light, perishing without the gospel, and they need the only remedy that God has ever provided–the gift of His Son.

Missionaries everywhere love this passage. Christian workers and Sunday school teachers in heathen lands find in this beautiful portion the love of God, the gift of Christ, and the ministry of the Spirit, filling all desires and meeting all the needs of human hearts.

The missionary urged us to be like Christ, who though He was rich, yet for our sakes made Himself poor, that we who are poor might become rich.

Most missionaries who go out into the Lord's harvest fleld, go out with John 3:16, and this verse is one of the very first to be translated into the native language.

The Chum Was Won

On a Wednesday evening, I was addressing a group the occasion of their annual city convention. It was during their "Win My Chum" week, and I was seeking to instruct the officers in the blessed and glorious art of soul-winning, so that they might win their chums during that special campaign. The text for the evening was John 3:16. I was showing the group how to explain this verse to their chums, and thus make the way of salvation clear to any friend who was in the dark.

As I reached the fourth phrase in the passage, a young lady rose suddenly in the very center of the congregation and raising her hand said, "Wait a moment, Dr. Wilson, may I interrupt you by asking a question?"

"Certainly," I replied, "speak your heart freely."

"Do you mean to tell us, or to tell me, that if I accept the Lord Jesus Christ right now, I will be a saved woman and will never perish?" I assured her that this was the case and read the verse again, emphasizing the fourth phrase, "should not perish."

She listened attentively, and when I had finished she at once announced to those assembled: "I accept this gift of God right now. I never knew before that salvation was a blessing to be possessed in this life. I see from this verse, John 3:16, that Christ may become mine immediately. I therefore accept Him and I believe I am a saved woman."

This testimony produced a blessed result in the audience and stirred every heart. How quickly the light of this passage brought this friend out of darkness into the light, and out of bondage into glorious liberty!

CHAPTER XVII

UNUSUAL DISTRIBUTIONS OF JOHN 3:16

PERHAPS no verse in the Bible has been distributed so widely in print and in so many ways as John 3:16. Let me mention a few of them.

On Mirrors

A banker in New York had a great desire to get the gospel to the soldiers at Sandy Hook, but was not permitted to carry the message to them in person. But his longing desire to help these men was not to be easily thwarted, so he called on a firm which manufactured advertising novelties and had them make several thousand small mirrors about three inches in diameter. On the celluloid back of each of these mirrors he had printed the words of John 3:16. Beneath the words of this inscription was written, "If you want to see who it is that God loves and for whom He gave His Son, look on the other side." These mirrors were distributed among the soldiers with the permission of the officers, and thus each man looking into the mirror would see the object of God's love and the one whom the Saviour came to save.

On Feathers

An enterprising tract distributor conceived the idea of passing out tracts without giving the recipient the opportunity to refuse. He called upon a firm which made advertising novelties and had them print John 3:16 upon feathers taken from the wings of the chicken. These were first dyed in bright colors and then the quill was fastened in a cockle-burr. The verse was printed in plain, black type on the feather so it could be easily read.

This friend then went around through the various fairs and groups of people on the street, sticking the cockle-burr to the clothes of the people whom he met. Of course, it was so attractive looking and so unusual in its appearance, that those who pulled the burr from the clothes stopped to read the message, and many of them were carried home for souvenirs.

On Signboards

Two farmer boys felt called of God to spread the gospel, but realized their inability to preach and their lack of opportunity to learn. They therefore had a large number of small signboards made. These were about 14" x 20". They were painted white, and then with a stencil John 3:16 was printed on them in large, readable type.

The boys had an old automobile which they loaded with these signs and started for California. They carried hammers and nails and a ten-foot ladder. As they journeyed, they nailed up these signs in prominent places along the way. At a sharp turn in the road, a sign would be placed so the motorist would read it as he slowed up in turning the corner. In the heart of the desert, a sign would be placed on some lone tree or planted on the top of a small knoll near the road. Other signs were shipped to widely-scattered -towns, so they could be picked up while in route. Thus on the way to California by one route, and all the way back by another, John 3: 16 was prominently brought to the attention of the traveler.

On Medals

A certain church in Kansas City has a medal the size of a silver dollar, made of aluminum, which bears on one side the name of the church and its address with the words "COME TO" in the center. On the reverse side of this medal John 3:16 is printed in full. On each Sunday morning, visitors in the Sunday school, who are there for the first time. are invited to rise after which four small children quickly carry to each one who is standing one of these medals as a souvenir of their visit and a request to return. John 3:16 is thus presented to each visiting friend.

On Lead Pencils

In order to reach business men, bankers, merchants, grocers, employees, and hundreds of others who use pencils, a servant of God had produced a very neat automatic pencil with John 3:16 printed on the body of the pencil, so that each time it is used this verse gives its message to the owner.

On an Orphanage

An orphan home was named "The John 3:16 Home." The children were called John 3:16. When one of these precious little boys was badly injured on the street, he told the officer that his name was John 3:16 and that he lived at John 3:16. This was a puzzle to the policeman, but the boy was taken to the hospital. In his delirium he could only tell them of John 3:16. Through his simple testimony, the nurse was led to look up the passage and to accept the Saviour.

On Pocket Knives

This verse has been widely distributed among children by the imprint of those words upon pocket knives. No one will throw away a good knife, for a knife is so often used. Every time it is taken from the pocket, this lovely verse sings its song of love and grace into the heart of the one who possesses it.

On Many Objects

On brass tablets, on plaques of clay, on blocks of granite, on rolls of leather, in tracts and books, this verse has proclaimed its love story to millions on earth.

It may be found on brass and iron, on aluminum and gold and silver, on parchment and linen. This story of God's love has found its way on many materials which have been commandeered to carry its message to perishing men.

It has been engraved in such small compass that a magnifying glass is required to read its inscription. It has been sung to a host of tunes. It has been memorized by children for public speaking. It has been proclaimed by the preacher in every clime and nation. It has been translated into over 900 languages and dialects.

SOME "DON'TS" FOR SOUL WINNERS

1. Don't think that everybody knows the meaning of John 3:16. Many of them have never studied it. Have them read it slowly.
2. Don't tell your friend that believing John 3:16 will save the soul. Christ alone can save.
3. Don't say to anyone, "If you believe John 3:16, you will have everlasting life." There are those who believe the statement, but never have experienced the gift in their own hearts.
4. Don't forget to apply each phrase personally to the heart of the one to whom you are speaking.
5. Don't put words in the mouth of the friend when using John 3:16, and mistake that for a conversion.
6. Don't ask questions about John 3:16 which can be answered with "Yes" or "No." You will probably not win the soul, but you will make a hypocrite.
7. Don't forget to differentiate between believing about Christ, and believing in or on Christ, as you explain the verse.
8. Don't be satisfied with leaving the verse with your friend, but be sure that you leave Christ Jesus with him.
9. Don't look for a mental conversion or admission concerning the truth of this verse, but look for the

light of life in the verse, as your friend enters into the personal blessing of the truth of it.

10.   Don't use this verse until you know that the soul desires a Saviour. Only those who feel the need of a gift will be interested in knowing about the gift of God, or be willing to receive it.

11.   Don't forget that this verse may be applied to a Christian, for the life of the Christian needs to be preserved from failure and ruin, and this can only be assured through a daily, living faith in Christ Jesus.

12.   Don't forget that this verse may be used as a missionary appeal. We should follow the example of the Father in loving lost men and then giving Christ to them.

13.   Don't forget that this verse may be used as a test in the spiritual life of another, to see whether he is really born again. If he has really believed in Christ Jesus, then he will have eternal life and this life will be manifested in ways that may be recognized by others.

14.   Don't forget that this verse brings God the Father immediately to our attention, for we are apt to neglect Him in telling about the Lord Jesus. The sinner should know that God is interested in His salvation.

15.   Don't forget that this verse may be used as a warning to lost men, for those who do not believe

in the Son will perish eternally. Their lives will perish here and their souls will perish hereafter.

16.   Don't forget that John 3:16 brings an unanswerable argument to the Unitarian, the Christian Scientist, the followers of Unity, and others who deny that there is a personal God and that Christ Jesus is a real person.

17.   Don't forget that this passage contains a sweet word of comfort to the sorrowing, who because of misfortune may feel that God does not love them as He should.

18.   Don't forget to rely upon the Holy Spirit, as you present John 3:16 to the saint or to the sinner, and trust Him to illumine the mind, quicken the heart, and impart the gift of eternal life.

The MOODY COLPORTAGE LIBRARY

A series of books by well-known Christian authors, undenominational, thoroughly evangelical, for all classes of readers. All uniform in size and style, attractive paper covers, 4¾ x 6¾ inches. 20 cents each.

1 All of Grace. C. H. Spurgeon
2 The Way to God. D. L. Moody
3 Pleasure and Profit in Bible Study. D. L. Moody
4 Life, Warfare and Victory. Whittle
5 Heaven. D. L. Moody
6 Prevailing Prayer. D. L. Moody
7 The Way of Life. Various authors
8 Secret Power. D. L. Moody
9 To the Work. D. L. Moody
10 According to Promise. C. H. Spurgeon
11 Bible Characters. D. L. Moody
13 "And Peter." J. W. Chapman
15 Light on Life's Duties. F. B. Meyer
18 The Good Shepherd. Life of Christ
19 Good Tidings. Talmage and others
20 Sovereign Grace. D. L. Moody
21 Select Sermons. D. L. Moody
23 Nobody Loves Me. Mrs. O. F. Walton
24 The Empty Tomb. Various authors
26 Sowing and Reaping. D. L. Moody
28 "Probable" Sons. Story. Amy LeFeuvre
30 Good News. Robert Boyd
32 The Secret of Guidance. F. B. Meyer
34 The Second Coming of Christ
40 The Power of a Surrendered Life, or Kadesh-Barnea. J. W. Chapman
42 Whiter Than Snow and Little Dot—Stories. Mrs. O. F. Walton
44 The Overcoming Life. D. L. Moody
46 A Royal Exile. T. D. Talmage
48 The Prodigal. Various authors
49 The Spirit-Filled Life. John MacNeil
50 Jessica's First Prayer. Hesba Stretton
51 The Christ-Life for the Self-Life. Meyer
54 Absolute Surrender. Andrew Murray
56 What is Faith? Spurgeon, Moody, etc.
57 Christie's Old Organ—A Story. Walton
58 Naaman the Syrian. A. B. Mackay
60 Weighed and Wanting—On the Ten Commandments. D. L. Moody
61 The Crew of the Dolphin. Hesba Stretton
63 Meet for the Master's Use. F. B. Meyer
64 Our Bible. C. Leach and R. A. Torrey
65 Alone in London. Hesba Stretton
66 Moody's Anecdotes
69 Children of the Bible
70 The Power of Pentecost. Thomas Waugh
71 Men of the Bible. D. L. Moody
72 A Peep Behind the Scenes. O. F. Walton
73 The School of Obedience. A. Murray
74 Home Duties. R. T. Cross
76 Moody's Stories
78 The Robber's Cave—A Story. A.L.O.E.
81 Thoughts for Quiet Hour. Moody
83 The Shorter Life of D. L. Moody. Vol. I. P. D. Moody and A. P. Fitt
85 The Revival of a Dead Church. Len G. Broughton
86 Moody's Latest Sermons
87 A Missionary Penny—A Story. L.C.W.
88 Calvary's Cross. Spurgeon, Whittle, etc.
89 How to Pray. R. A. Torrey
90 Little King Davie—Story. Nellie Hellis
91 Short Talks. D. L. Moody
93 Pilgrim's Progress. John Bunyan
96 Kept for the Master's Use. Havergal
98 Back to Bethel. F. B. Meyer
100 Up from Sin. Len G. Broughton
102 Popular Amusements and the Christian Life. P. W. Sinks
104 Answers to Prayer, from George Muller's Narratives

105 The Way Home. D. L. Moody
109 Life of David Livingstone. Mrs. J. H. Worcester, Jr.
114 First Words to Young Christians. Boyd
115 Rosa's Quest—A Story. Anna P. Wright
116 Difficulties in the Bible. R. A. Torrey
119 Practical and Perplexing Questions Answered. R. A. Torrey
120 Satan and the Saint. James M. Gray
123 Salvation from Start to Finish. James M. Gray
125 Life in a Look. Maurice S. Baldwin
126 Burton Street Folks. Anna P. Wright
127 Bible Problems Explained. J. M. Gray
128 Papers on Our Lord's Coming. "C.H.M."
129 The Christian: His Creed and Conduct. William Evans
130 Intercessory Prayer. J. G. K. McClure
131 From Death Unto Life. J. H. Brookes
132 Ruth, the Moabitess. Henry Moorhouse
134 Forty-Eight Bernard Street. Mrs. S. R. Graham Clark
135 Deliverance from the Penalty and Power of Sin. O. R. Palmer
136 Mrs. Mary's Go-Tell. Graham Clark
137 Bird's-Eye Bible Study. A. Patterson
138 "I Cried, He Answered"
141 Later Evangelistic Sermons. Biederwolf
142 Phil Tyler's Opportunity. F. E. Burnham
143 Sunday Night Talks. J. C. Massee
144 The Christ We Know. A. C. Gaebelein
145 Five "Musts" of the Christian Life. F. B. Meyer
146 The New Life in Christ Jesus. C. L. Scofield
147 Problems of the Prayer Life. Buswell
148 When the Song of the Lord Began. W. E. Biederwolf
149 The Christian Life and How to Live It. W. H. Griffith Thomas
150 Where Is the Lord God of Elijah? E. K. Cox
151 The Faith that Wins. Roy T. Brumbaugh
152 God's Way of Holiness. H. Bonar
153 Souls Set Free. Mission Field Miracles
154 Thinking with God. Norman H. Camp
155 "Charge That to My Account." H. A. Ironside
156 Vera Dickson's Triumph. Sara C. Palmer
157 Competing Artists. Sara C. Palmer
158 The Antidote to Christian Science. James M. Gray
159 Is the Bible the Word of God? W. Graham Scroggie
160 And God Spake These Words. W. H. Griffith Thomas
161 Methods of Bible Study. W. H. Griffith Thomas
162 The Romance of a Doctor's Visits. Walter L. Wilson
163 The Little Shepherd. Anna Potter Wright
164 God's Picked Young Men. Henry K. Pasma
165 The Cross of Christ. James H. Todd
166 By Ways Appointed. Briggs P. Dingman
167 Miracles in a Doctor's Life. Walter L. Wilson
168 The Living Christ. Will H. Houghton
169 Portraits of Christ in the Gospel of John. Harold Samuel Laird